DANISH YEARBOOK
OF
PHILOSOPHY

VOLUME 39

DANISH YEARBOOK OF PHILOSOPHY

VOLUME 39

2004

MUSEUM TUSCULANUM PRESS
UNIVERSITY OF COPENHAGEN 2005

Published for
Dansk Filosofisk Selskab
in cooperation with
the Philosophical Societies of Aarhus and Odense
and with financial support from
the Danish Research Council for the Humanities

*

EDITORIAL BOARD:

FINN COLLIN	JØRGEN HUGGLER	UFFE JUUL JENSEN
University of Copenhagen	Danish University of Education	University of Aarhus
Chairman		
SVEN ERIK NORDENBO	STIG ANDUR PEDERSEN	ERICH KLAWONN
University of Copenhagen	Roskilde University Centre	Odense University
HANS SIGGAARD JENSEN	MOGENS PAHUUS	LARS GUNDERSEN
Copenhagen Business School	Aalborg University	University of Aarhus

*

Articles for consideration and all editorial communications should be sent in three copies to:
Danish Yearbook of Philosophy
University of Copenhagen, Department of Philosophy
Njalsgade 80, DK 2300 Copenhagen S, Denmark

Business communications, including subscriptions and orders for reprints, should
be addressed to the publishers:
MUSEUM TUSCULANUM PRESS
Njalsgade 94
DK 2300 Copenhagen S
Denmark

*

© 2004 DANISH YEARBOOK OF PHILOSOPHY
COPENHAGEN, DENMARK
PRINTED IN DENMARK
BY SPECIAL-TRYKKERIET VIBORG

ISBN 87-635-0289-5
ISSN 0070-2749

CONTENTS

Shaun Gallagher: *Consciousness and Free Will* 7

Søren Overgaard: *The Private Language Argument and Externalism* 17

Morten Ebbe Juul Nielsen: *Out of Harm's Way?* 49

Nikolaj Nottelmann: *Foresight and Blameworthiness for Action Consequences* 67

Stig Alstrup Rasmussen: *Reality Confounded: Discussion Review* 75

CONSCIOUSNESS AND FREE WILL

SHAUN GALLAGHER

Department of Philosophy and Cognitive Science
University of Central Florida
gallaghr@mail.ucf.edu

Abstract: I argue against epiphenomenalist views that consciousness is part of and has an effect on the system in which action is generated. Those who deny free will based on recent results in neuroscience are looking for it at the wrong level of explanation. Free will is not about subpersonal neuronal processes, muscular activation, or basic bodily movements, but about contextualized actions in a system that is larger than many contemporary philosophers of mind, psychologists, and neuroscientists consider.

Here is an argument from (an imperfect) analogy, inspired by some things that John Searle (1984) has said about consciousness and emergence. Imagine that a group of scientists maintain that water is not really liquid because at the molecular level of H_2 and O there is no liquidity. It seems to me that this is imperfectly analogous to the recent scientific arguments that free will is an illusion. There are scientists who maintain that conscious control over our actions is an illusion because at the neuronal level where these actions are caused, there is no conscious control, and hence, in the physical system responsible for action control, there is no free will.

Clearly, we would say that the first group of scientists are silly because they are looking for liquidity at the wrong level – that is, at a level where it has not yet emerged as a property of water. If these scientists respond by accusing us of invoking some magical explanation, we could rightly answer with a scientific and purely physical explanation of how liquidity emerges from specific super-molecular structures.[1] Could we do something similar in the second case? That's what I would like to try to do in this paper. First, I want to argue that the scientists and philosophers who argue that free will is an illusion (e.g., Claxton, 1999; Wegner 2002; Frith 2002)[2] are looking for free will in the wrong place, or at the wrong level of explanation. Indeed, even those who try to work out arguments against these "illusioneers" often try to construct arguments that appeal to the wrong level of explanation. Second I want to suggest how we can rightly respond to these theorists without appeal to magic, but with a scientific, naturalistic explanation that shows the reality of free will.

In general terms the notion of free will that I will be arguing for is closer to a compatibilist concept than to a libertarian concept. Still, without appealing to quantum levels of explanation, I will provide reasons to doubt that the physical system at stake here is fully deterministic. Further, the concept of free will that I will defend is no more "Libetarian" than libertarian. Benjamin Libet, whose experiments are close to the center of the recent debates, offers an anti-illusioneer account of free will that is framed at the same (wrong) level of explanation as the illusioneer account.

The wrong level

Let's start with the experiments conducted by Libet (1985; 1992; 1996; Libet et al. 1983) that have motivated much of the current discussion. These experiments suggest that motor action itself, and the sense of agency that comes along with it, depend on brain events that we do not control, and that happen before our conscious decision to act. In Libet's experiments an array of surface electrodes are attached to subjects to monitor brain activity. The subjects are then asked to place their hands on a table top and to flick their wrists whenever they want to. The brain activity leading up to the movement lasts between 500-1000 msecs (0.5 to 1 sec). Just before the subject flicks their wrist, there is 50 msec of activity in the motor nerves descending from motor cortex to the wrist. This is preceded by several hundred (up to 800) msecs of brain activity known as the readiness potential (RP). To ascertain when subjects were first aware of their decision to move their wrists, Libet designed a large clock that allowed subjects to report fractions of a second. Using the clock, subjects were asked to indicate the precise time at which they decided to move their wrist, or were first aware of the urge to do so. The results indicated that on average, 350 msecs before subjects are conscious of deciding (or having an urge) to move, their brains are already working on the motor processes that will result in the movement. Before they know it, the readiness potential is already underway, and they are preparing to move. Thus, so-called voluntary acts are 'initiated by unconscious cerebral processes before conscious intention appears' (Libet 1985). What we call "decisions" are made by the brain, which then enacts its decisions in a nonconscious fashion, on a subpersonal level. But the brain also inventively tricks us into thinking that we consciously decide matters and that our actions are personal events.

This kind of evidence clearly raises the question of whether free will is nothing more than an epiphenomenal illusion. "The initiation of the freely voluntary act appears to begin in the brain unconsciously, well before the person consciously knows he wants to act. Is there, then, any role for conscious will in the performance of a voluntary act?" (Libet 1999: 51). Thus, for example, Wegner and others argue that these experiments provide evidence that free will is an illusion. Libet himself, however, thinks that we can save free will – because there is still approximately 150 msecs of brain activity left after we become conscious of our decision, and before we move. So, he suggests, we have time to consciously veto the movement (1985, 2003).

I will outline two reasons why I think that both the illusioneer and the Libetarian arguments are misguided because they frame the question on the wrong level of analysis. First, free will cannot be squeezed into timeframes of 150-350 msecs; free will is a longer-term phenomenon that depends on consciousness, and in this respect the sense of agency is more than just an accessory – or so I will argue. Second, the notion of free will does not apply primarily to abstract motor processes that make up intentional actions – rather it applies to intentional, purposive actions themselves, described at the highest pragmatic level of description.

First, in regard to timeframe, we must consider that decisions are not confined to the spur of the moment – and specifically, they are not momentary. To the extent that decisions are momentary or fully spontaneous, they may not be as free as we think. More obviously, there is a distinction between fast, automatic reflex action and slower voluntary action. Let's take an example. At time T a snake moves in the grass next to my feet.

- T+150 msecs. Before I realize what is happening, my amygdala is activated.
- T+200 msecs. Without a sense of agency – I jump and move several yards away. Here, the entire set of movements can be explained purely in terms of neurons firing and muscles contracting, etc.

Once I become aware of what is happening (e.g., at T+1000 msecs.), my next move is not of the same sort.
- T+4000 msecs. I recognize the snake as harmless.
- T+5000 msecs. I decide to catch it.
- T+5150 msecs. I take a step back and *voluntarily* reach for the snake.

In some sense we might say that my choice to reach for the snake is momentary, since at some point in time (T+4900 msecs) I had not decided to catch the snake; some 100 msecs later I had decided. Still, what goes into this decision involves awareness of what has just happened plus recognition of the snake as harmless. At T+5150 msecs. I take a step back and reach for the snake. We could focus in a Libetian way on this movement and say that at T+4650 msecs, without my awareness, processes in my brain were already underway to prepare for my reaching action, before I had even decided to catch the snake. So, what seemed to be my decision was actually predetermined by my brain. But this ignores the context defined by the larger timeframe – which involves previous movement and a conscious recognition of the snake. Furthermore it is likely that things don't go as fast as I've portrayed, and that I would have to wait for an opportune moment to grab the snake. Perhaps, then, I don't actually reach for the snake until 10 seconds after my decision to catch it. Even if Libet would say that an extra decision would have to be made to initiate the reach precisely at that time, isn't that decision already under the control of the initial decision? Voluntary acts are normally spread out over a larger timeframe than experimental milliseconds.

I have argued elsewhere (Gallagher 2005; Gazzaniga and Gallagher 2000) that reflex movements and voluntary actions depend on a very basic biological function found in all living organisms: the feedback loop. In nature, even feedback loops that are purely automatic require time. Feedback loops that involve conscious deliberation require an extended duration, that is, one stretched out over at least several seconds, and are experienced as such.

The issue of extended timeframe suggests a second reason why the Libetian analysis misses the proper level of description relevant to free will. Despite a long tradition of discussing free will by appealing to examples of bodily movements, e.g., "Look how I can freely raise my hand" (see, for instance, Chisholm 1964; Searle 1984 – this type of example has become almost ubiquitous, and I simply can't list all the recent papers that use precisely this example as paradigmatic), free will is primarily about contextualized and complex intentional actions, and not about the simple bodily movements that subtend intentional actions. In other words, the kinds of actions that we freely decide are not the sort of bodily movements described by Libet's experiments. Indeed, in cases of intentional actions, because we ordinarily pay no attention to the details of our bodily movements, and rarely make any explicit decisions about them, directing attention to such movements in experimental situations is an involuted form of action. One way to put this is to say that we normally characterize our intentional actions on the highest pragmatic level possible. If I am reaching to catch the snake and you stop and ask what I'm doing, which one of the following descriptions is the most appropriate?

> I am activating my neurons.
> I am flexing my muscles.
> I am moving my arm.
> I am reaching and grasping.
> I am trying to catch the snake.

My decision, and so my free will, is directly tied to the last description listed, not to the other descriptions. In some sense, of course, as I reach to catch the snake, I am doing all of the above. But my free will is not exercised for the sake of neurons, muscles, arm movements, or graspings. It is, in this case, exercised for snake catching. In this regard, the following complaint, as Velmans (2002, p. 8) points out, completely misses the point. "One is not conscious of one's own brain/body processing. So how could there be conscious control of such processing?"

Voluntary actions and the exercise of free will are not about neurons, muscles, body parts, or even movement – all of which play some part in what is happening, and for the most part, are nonconsciously carried along by (and are intentional because of) my decision to catch the snake (or to participate in an experiment, etc.). Free will is best described at the personal level in regard to intentional action. To look for it amongst neurons and bodily movements is to look for it in the wrong place; to characterize it as "a mediating executive mental process, which somehow puts the bodily parts into action" (Zhu 2003: 64), is to misconstrue the phenomenon. Bodily movements are simply not the "prototype" (Ibid.) of free action. The subpersonal aspects of body-schematic control are like the vehicle to the volitional content. Just as we don't say that the neurons that generate visual red are themselves red, likewise, we shouldn't say that the bodily movements that carry my freely chosen intentional action are themselves freely chosen, at least in any direct sense. I don't choose to take a drink and then, in addition, choose to extend my arm and shape my grasp ... nor *vice versa*. In a derivative fashion one might say that in taking a drink I am freely extending my arm, etc., but only in the same way that one might say that the neurons activated when I see red are the "red neurons," without meaning that the neurons are *literally* red. The reach and grasp, the muscle extension, the neuronal activations are not freely chosen *per se*. This would be a severe involution of embodied conscious experience.

This does not mean that brain events and body-schematic processes that work on a subpersonal level are simply irrelevant to free will. Such processes, including the kind of neurological events described by Libet, are important insofar as they support intentional action and are structured and regulated by relevant intentional goals. In addition, as studies of deafferented subjects suggest, precisely to the degree that we are not required to consciously deliberate about bodily movement or such things as autonomic processes, our deliberation can be more easily directed at the more meaningful level of intentional action. In some limited ways, the loss of a body schema and the disruption of automatic processes, rob a person of a degree of freedom (see, e.g., Gallagher and Cole 1995).

A non-magical account of free will

What we call free will, I maintain, cannot be conceived as something *purely* subpersonal, or as some first-person instantaneous feeling, an event that takes place in a knife-edge moment located between being undecided and being decided. If that were the case it would completely dissipate in the milliseconds between brain events and our conscious awareness. If by free will we mean what it means for common sense realism, or for most of the Western philosophical tradition, roughly, the ability to choose and control our actions, and to act otherwise than we do,[3] then free will involves at least the temporally extended processing involved in the feedback of perceptual consciousness,[4] the "looping effects" (Hacking 1995) that can be transformed and enhanced by the introduction of deliberative consciousness. This means that the conscious sense of agency, even if it starts out as an accessory experience generated by the brain, is itself a real force that counts in the formation of our future action. It contributes to the freedom of action, and bestows responsibility on the agent.

Daniel Dennett (2003) has addressed these issues in his recent work *Freedom Evolves*. On his view, the processes that constitute free will may be purely subpersonal, distributed brain processes, and need not be conscious or depend on conscious decision. He does insist, however, that free will requires an extended timeframe.

> Once you distribute the work done ... in both space and time in the brain, you have to distribute the moral agency around as well. You are not out of the loop, you *are* the loop. You are that large. You are not an extentionless point. What you do and what you are *incorporates* all these things that happen and is not something separate from them. (Dennett 2003: 242)

In this regard, Dennett thinks I have part (but only part) of it right.

> One commentator on Libet who gets close is Sean [sic] Gallagher: 'I think that this problem can be solved as long as we do not think of free will as a momentary act. Once we understand that deliberation and decision are processes that are spread out over time, even, in some cases, very short amounts of time, then there is plenty of room for conscious components that are more than accessories after the fact' ([Gazzaniga and] Gallagher 1998). But, then he [Gallagher] goes on to say that if the feedback is all unconscious, it will be 'deterministic' but if it is conscious, it won't be. Cartesian thinking dies hard. (Dennett 2003: 242n3).

I think that Dennett is right to enlarge the system, and I don't disagree with Dennett concerning the role played by nonconscious elements (and of course I reject the charge of Cartesianism). As Velmans (2002, p. 20) puts it: "We are *both* the pre-conscious generating process *and* the conscious results" (also see Velmans 2003). But I think we are even larger than either Dennett or Velmans think – we are not just what happens in our brains, and/or the pure results of such happenings. The 'loop' that we *are* extends through and is limited by our bodily capabilities, into the surrounding environment, which is social as well as physical; and it is a loop that feeds back through our conscious experience into the decisions we make.

The neurological processes described by Libet, Dennett, and others, are, as I have indicated, essential to the exercise of free will. As much as these processes enable and limit my action, however, they are also structured and regulated by my intentional goals. When I decide to reach for the snake all of the appropriate neurological events line up, and my physical movements fall into place. In carrying out my action, no conscious deliberation about bodily movement is normally required. I have to keep my eye on the snake; I don't have to keep my eye on my reaching hand. Underlying body schematic processes – readiness potentials, motor signals, proprioceptive feedback – allow for this transparency of the body-in-action, and they are part of what it means to carry out the deliberated action (Eilan 2003; Gallagher 2005).

If, however, we think of intentional action as *solely* the product of these subintentional events, based on feedback that is *all* unconscious, made possible by a committee of "mindless robots" (Dennett 2003, p. 2), or possible for a system only as large as a brain in a vat, we fail to recognize the true size of the system that we are. The temporal framework for the exercise of free will is, at a minimum, the temporal framework that allows for the system to be informed by consciousness – complex perceptual consciousness that allows me, for example, to recognize a snake as non-poisonous and as within my reach; and further, deliberative awareness that this is something that I want to get. Once events of conscious deliberation are included in the behavioral feedback loop certain things in the environment begin to matter to the agent; meaning comes into the picture; and conscious interpretation processes introduce temporally extended looping effects. The conscious deliberation of the agent, which likely involves memory and knowledge – cognitive schemas (e.g., about snakes) – rather than being epiphenomenal, has real effects on behavior. The reason that the act of reaching for the snake is not a reflex or involuntary action is that my conscious interpretation of the situation has an effect. To the extent that consciousness enters into the ongoing production of action, and contributes to the production of further action, *even if significant aspects of this production takes place nonconsciously*, it can shift the system and determine future responses. It is only in these contexts that the issue of free will is at stake. The discourse of free will is not tailored to issues that pertain to basic bodily movements, despite the attempt of many philosophers to frame the question in these terms. Indeed, to talk about free will in such mechanical terms is to adopt the Cartesian question: how does the mind move my body. Rather, the issue of free will is an issue only in the realm of action, and action is never reducible to mechanical bodily movement.

Free will is neither magical nor absolute. It is not magical because it is possible to give an explanation of it in terms of a physical system that includes brain, body, environment, and the experiences generated in their interaction. It is not absolute because it is limited by the physical conditions of the system, including current brain processes (and physical brain structures) that have been shaped by prior experience, by genetically guided development, as well as by affordances that are neither arbitrary nor purely objective facts, since they are defined only relative to the possibilities of the system.[5] These things shape our experiences and our decisions, which then feed back into the system to shape or modify our actions. Free will is exercised within this larger system where meaningful actions can develop.

Just as liquidity is not explainable purely in terms of individual molecules, free will is not explainable purely in terms of neurons or bodily movements. On the one hand, it would be silly to expect Wegner and Velmans to find a free will that looks real, when they look only at these subpersonal levels. On the other hand, the compatibilist free will that Libet, Dennett, Velmans and others find is either too fleeting or too automatic to make a big difference in what looks like a strongly deterministic system at the same subpersonal levels. One implication of understanding free will as something that emerges in a larger system of intentional action, a system that includes brain, body, physical and social environments, and the looping effects of consciousness, is that it introduces some indeterminacy into the system as a whole, just at the level where free will is relevant. Although in certain aspects the system itself determines how inputs are shaped, and how they are delivered (how they become conscious), already dressed up with meaning, in just this way the system opens itself up to indeterminate possibilities. All inputs to the system are not decided in advance, and, human action being what it is, the result is such that one cannot predict precisely what the outcome will be.*

Notes

1. For some important reservations about the notion of ontological emergence, however, see Bitbol (in press).
2. Frith (2002) states, in apparent sympathy with Wegner (2002), "in a sense our experience of controlling our own actions is illusory. ... All we can actually experience is the contingency between thought and action" (p. 483). See Wegner and Wheatley (1999).
3. As Bernard Williams (1995, p. 5) puts it, "something to the effect that agents sometimes act voluntarily, and that when they do so they have a real choice between more than one course of action; or more than one course is open to them; or it is up to them which of several actions they perform."
4. See Eilan (2003) for a perceptual theory of what makes our action conscious.
5. Accordingly, free will should not be thought of as an all or nothing phenomenon, but a matter of degree, not unlike what experimental science has recently shown about the sense of agency (Farrer et al. 2003; Brøsted Sørensen 2005).
* Editorial note: This paper was to have been presented at a cenference in Copenhagen in May 2004. Unfortunately, the author had to cancel his participation in the event, but kindly agreed to make the manuscript available to *Danish Yearbook of Philosophy* instead.

References

Bitbol, M. (in press). Ontology, matter, and emergence. *Phenomenology and the Cognitive Sciences.*

Brøsted Sørensen, J. 2005. The Alien Hand Experiment. *Phenomenology and the Cognitive Sciences* 4 (1).

Chisholm, R. 1964. Human freedom and the self. The Langley Lecture, 1964. University of Kansas. Reprinted in J. Feinberg and R. Shafer-Landau (eds.), *Reason and Responsibility: Readings in Some Basic Problems of Philosophy*, 11th Edition (492-99). New York: Wadsworth, 2002.

Claxton, G. 1999. Whodunnit? Unpicking the 'seems' of free will. *Journal of Consciousness Studies* 6 (8-9): 99-113.

Dennett, D. 2003. *Freedom Evolves*. New York: Viking.

Eilan, N. 2003. The explanatory role of consciousness in action. In S. Maasen, W. Prinz, and G. Roth (eds.). *Voluntary Action: Brains, Minds, and Sociality* (188-201). Oxford: Oxford University Press.

Farrer, C., Franck, N. Georgieff, N. Frith, C.D. Decety, J. and Jeannerod, M. 2003. Modulating the experience of agency: a positron emission tomography study. *NeuroImage* 18 (2003) 324–333

Frith, C. 2002. Attention to action and awareness of other minds. *Consciousness and Cognition*, 11: 481-487.

Gallagher, S. 2005. *How the Body Shapes the Mind*. Oxford: Oxford University Press.

Gallagher, S. and Cole, J. 1995. Body schema and body image in a deafferented subject. *Journal of Mind and Behavior,* 16: 369-390.

Gazzaniga, M. and Gallagher, S. 1998. A neuronal Platonist: An interview with Michael Gazzaniga. *Journal of Consciousness Studies* 5: 706-717.

Hacking, I. 1995. The looping effects of human kinds. In D. Sperber, D. Premack and A. J. Premack (eds.), *Causal Cognition: A Multidisciplinary Debate* (pp. 351-383) New York: Oxford University Press.

Libet, B. 1985. Unconscious cerebral initiative and the role of conscious will in voluntary action. *Behavioral and Brain Sciences*, 8: 529-66.

Libet, B. 1992. The neural time-factor in perception, volition, and free will. *Revue de Métaphysique et de Morale,* 2: 255-72.

Libet, B. 1996, Neural time factors in conscious and unconscious mental functions. In S. R. Hammeroff et al. (eds.), *Toward a Science of Consciousness: The First Tucson Discussions and Debates*. Cambridge, MA: MIT Press.

Libet, B. 1999. Do we have free will? *Journal of Consciousness Studies,* 6 (8-9): 47-57.

Libet, B. 2003. Can conscious experience affect brain activity? *Journal of Consciousness Studies,* 10 (12): 24-28.

Libet, B., Gleason, C. A., Wright, E. W. and Perl, D. K. 1983. Time of conscious intention to act in relation to cerebral activities (readiness potential): The unconscious initiation of a freely voluntary act. *Brain*, 102: 193-224.

Searle, J. 1984. *Minds, Brains, and Science*. Cambridge, MA: Harvard University Press.

Velmans, M. (2002) "How Could Conscious Experiences Affect Brains," *Journal of Consciousness Studies*, **9** (11), pp. 3-29.

Velmans, M. 2003. Preconscious free will. *Journal of Consciousness Studies* 10 (12): 42-61.

Williams, B. 1995. *Making Sense of Humanity*. New York: Cambridge University Press.

Wegner, D. 2002. *The Illusion of Conscious Will*. Cambridge, MA: MIT Press.

Wegner, D. & Wheatley, T. 1999. Apparent mental causation – sources of experience of will. *American Psychology* 54: 480-92.

Zhu, J. 2003. Reclaiming volition: An alternative interpretation of Libet's experiments. *Journal of Consciousness Studies,* 10 (11): 61-77.

THE PRIVATE LANGUAGE ARGUMENT
AND EXTERNALISM

SØREN OVERGAARD

Danish National Research Foundation: Center for Subjectivity Research
University of Copenhagen
Købmagergade 46
DK-1150 Copenhagen K
E-mail: sov@cfs.ku.dk

I. Introduction

Can such things as grasping the meaning of a word, perceiving that a rabbit is running by, or suddenly remembering that one has to do the laundry be constituted *solely* by whatever goes on "inside" an individual person? Or does the environment of the individual play an important role as well? These are the issues at stake in the debate(s) between so-called semantic "internalists" and semantic "externalists". A paradigmatic internalist is one who answers, "Yes" to the first question, and consequently "No" to the second. An externalist, on the other hand, is someone who maintains that the content of mental states and occurrences such as the ones mentioned is at least co-constituted by the nature of the individual's (physical and/or social) environment. So an internalist would typically claim that I could "think about water", for instance, no matter what my environment would be like (whether or not it contained a fluid, colorless substance with the chemical structure H_2O), indeed regardless of whether I was simply a brain in a vat[1] or a completely free-floating mind devoid of an environment altogether. Since "thinking about water" is just a psychological state (or a neurological state) in me, this state might obtain without anything "outside" being even remotely like I think it is, according to the internalist.[2] The externalist, however, would argue that I cannot think about *water* unless my environment is in a certain way. For instance, the externalist might claim that my environment has to contain some fluid, colorless and (more or less) tasteless substance that quenches thirst and behaves in various other relevant ways.

But in the real world, of course, things are often more complicated than such clear-cut oppositions allow for. Even given a general sympathy with, say, an externalist outlook, a question remains concerning what *type* of externalism one should prefer. The questions raised in the present paper precisely concern this. More precisely, the paper addresses some claims Gregory McCulloch makes about Wittgenstein and externalism. I aim to show, first, that Wittgenstein advocates some form of semantic externalism. In my attempt to show this I will be relying mainly on Wittgenstein's so-called "private language argument". Second, and most importantly, I want to discuss the *kind* of externalism Wittgenstein would be prepared to endorse. Referring again to the private language argument I try to show that it is wrong to suppose, as McCulloch does, that Wittgenstein's externalism can be made to harmonize with a strong metaphysical realism.

II. A Visit to Twin Earth

Let me first introduce a classical formulation of semantic externalism. It appears, although the word "externalism" does not, in Hilary Putnam's article "The Meaning of 'Meaning'". Putnam's main concern in this long and rather complicated paper is to refute certain dogmas in traditional philosophical semantics. In particular, Putnam argues that we should give up the idea that "knowing the meaning of a term is just a matter of being in a certain psychological state" (Putnam 1975, p. 219), where "psychological state" should be understood as involving what Putnam calls "the assumption of methodological solipsism".[3] The latter is "the assumption that no psychological state, properly so called, presupposes the existence of any individual other than the subject to whom that state is ascribed" (Putnam 1975, p. 220).[4] In his efforts to show that "the psychological state of the individual speaker does not determine 'what he means'" (Putnam 1975, p. 270), Putnam introduces a (by now famous) thought experiment. Suppose that in a remote galaxy there is a planet very much like the Earth; so much like the Earth, in fact, that people speak English, and that each of us earthlings has his or her own *Doppelgänger* up there, who is psychologically (in the relevant sense) exactly like the earthly counterpart. Just like the Earth, this "Twin Earth" has its forests, oceans, mountain ranges, cities, and so forth. But here is a difference: Whereas what we call "water" here on earth has the chemical formula H_2O, what the Twin Earth inhabitants call "water" has a quite different formula that we might abbreviate XYZ. Twin Earth "water", however, is superficially indistinguishable from (Earth) water, and it plays exactly the same kinds of roles (quenching thirst, etc.). Suppose now that the pair of *Doppelgänger* Hilary (on Earth) and Twin Hilary (on Twin Earth) who have had completely parallel lives, including the same contact with (what they have learned to call) water, and who are in every "psychological"[5] respect perfect duplicates, both think they want "a glass of water". Putnam's point is that even if Hilary and Twin Hilary are psychologically type-identical they nevertheless *mean* something different when they talk or think about "water".

But why do we have to conclude that they mean something different? Why can't Putnam's opponents simply say that the two Hilarys *mean* the same when they say "water", even if it just so happens that the referent in each case is different? Or, to put it in Fregean terms, why can't we separate *Sinn* and *Bedeutung* and claim that *Sinn* (determined by psychological state) is what constitutes meaning? After all, when I say "I", and when you say "I", the referents (*Bedeutung*, extension) are different; but it would nevertheless be strange to claim that the *word* "I" *means* something different in the mouth of each speaker of English (if it did, how could I ever know what another speaker meant by it?). Now why can't it be the same with "water"? That is, why can't we just hold that the psychological type-identity of Hilary and Twin Hilary exclusively determines what they mean when they say "water" *because it determines the "Sinn"* of their words, which alone constitutes the *meaning* of those words?

Putnam grants that it is possible to take the line in question (Putnam 1975, pp. 234, 245-246). Yet he thinks it has certain obvious disadvantages. Suppose Hilary and Twin Hilary are both rather ignorant when it comes to their local flora. In particular, they do not have a very firm grasp of the words "beech" and "elm". They are unable to tell a beech from an elm, and in fact their understanding of *both* words can be adequately summed up in something like this: "a big deciduous tree". Again, the two Hilarys are "psychologically" indistinguishable when they say the word "elm". So according to the view that Putnam is opposing (the view that the psychological state of the individual speaker determines what he or she means), this would mean that the *Sinn* of the word "elm" would be the same for Hilary and Twin Hilary ("big deciduous tree"), and the *meaning* therefore also. But this does not seem right. First of all, the *meaning* that the word "elm" has – *for Hilary too*, when he uses it – is not so closely tied to *his* grasp of the word. Rather, it is connected more closely with the kind of grasp botanists and other more competent speakers of Hilary's linguistic community have of the word "elm". This latter grasp, in turn, seems to have a lot to do with the ability to determine what belongs to the extension or *Bedeutung* of the word, that is, the ability, for example, to tell whether a particular tree is a beech, or rather an elm or an oak. And, as Putnam points out, if the words "beech" and "elm" "are 'switched' on Twin Earth, then surely we would *not* say that 'elm' has the same meaning on Earth and Twin Earth", even if the two Hilarys have the same fuzzy grasp (what Putnam calls "concept") of "elm" and "beech" (namely, "big deciduous tree") (Putnam 1975, pp. 245-246).[6]

There are two sides to Putnam's claim here. The first concerns the role of other speakers. To illustrate the Putnamian case on this point, let us briefly transport the "switching" example back to Earth. Suppose Hilary and Twin Hilary speak the same language (call it "Germanic") with one little difference, which will become important.[7] They both have the same grasp or "concept" of the word "*Meer*". Let us say that the following description fits the concept of *Meer* that both Hilarys have: "a place with a lot of water". When saying *Meer* the two Hilarys are psychologically type-identical, and their "concept" is the same. Does the word have the same meaning of the word in the mouths of the two Hilarys? Well, suppose that in the western part of the Germanic territory, where Hilary lives, *Meer* refers to lakes, while in the east, where Twin Hilary lives, it refers to seas and oceans. Putnam's opponent would maintain that the psychological state determines meaning; thus, the two Hilarys *mean* the same thing when the utter the word, despite the different references. Putnam, however, would claim that what Hilary *means* when he utters the word is co-determined by his linguistic community. And surely this is right. The linguistic community has some role in fixing the *Bedeutung*, and it would seem counterintuitive in the case under consideration to refuse to let this matter to the *meaning* of the word. Whatever the psychological state and the "concept" that the western Hilary has – the word *Meer* in his mouth surely *means* something quite different from what it *means* in the mouth of his eastern *Doppelgänger*. We thus seem to reach the conclusion that individual "psychological state" and "concept" or "grasp" does not determine the meaning of a word. The linguistic community plays an important part too in fixing meaning. This is especially obvious when we look at terms, which the average speaker in a linguistic community cannot do much with. Presumably "molybdenum" and "elm" are examples of such words: when an average speaker uses them, she does so without a clear grasp of the criteria for something to be molybdenum or an elm. But she may do so because there is a "division of linguistic labor", such that there are others in the linguistic community (experts, or simply more competent speakers) who *do* know how to identify a piece of molybdenum and tell whether a given tree is an elm, a beech, or an oak (Putnam 1975, pp. 227-229).

Thus, this should establish the first part of Putnam's claim: *Meaning is co-determined by the linguistic community.*[8]

To appreciate the force of the second part of Putnam's claim, let us return to "natural kind" terms. Although Putnam resists the idea that natural kind terms should be construed as indexical in completely the same way as "I" or "here", he nevertheless thinks there is an implicit indexical component in such words. The meaning of such words is co-determined by "local" environmental samples. What *we* mean by "water" is paradigmatically the stuff that fills up *earthly* lakes and oceans: if anything else is to count as water (for us), it must bear "a certain similarity relation to the water *around here*" (Putnam 1975, p. 234). This should bring out the crucial lesson of the Twin Earth fiction, for there is a clear asymmetry between Earth and Twin Earth concerning the meaning of the (English, earthly) word "water". If we were to discover that the stuff that fills up earthly lakes and oceans had a slightly different chemical structure than hitherto assumed, we would not conclude that there after all was no water. We would rather conclude that *water* actually has a chemical structure slightly different from H_2O.[9] It is hard to imagine something that would count as a case in which all our earthly "water" was not *water*. Things are quite different for Twin Earth, however. If we would discover that the stuff we found up there in lakes and oceans had a different chemical structure than H20, then we *would* conclude that the fluid Twin Earth stuff was not water. It is thus very easy to imagine a case where "water" from another galaxy is not *water*. What the word "water" means, then, is not independent of the nature of the (local) environment. If the nature of paradigmatic local samples is discovered to be otherwise than hitherto thought, then the meaning of the word tends to follow that discovery ("water actually has *that* structure"). If more distant and peripheral samples are discovered to be different from what was expected (viz. something with the *same* nature as the local samples), the conclusion might well be that "this, although practically indistinguishable from water, isn't water after all". This second part of Putnam's claim can be formulated in the following way: *Meaning is co-determined by the external world.*[10]

So what does all this show? Putnam thinks it provides an important corrective to traditional philosophical semantics. As he ironically puts it, traditional theory of meaning ignores "only two contributions" to the meanings of our words: "the contribution of society and the contribution of the real world!" (Putnam 1975, p. 245; cf. p. 271). We might thus formulate Putnamian externalism in this way: *what a speaker means is not determined exclusively by his or her "psychological state" alone, but also by his or her (local) environment and linguistic community.*

III. "In-the-World Wittgensteinianism"

In his forceful and stimulating book *The Mind and Its World*, Gregory McCulloch provides a detailed defense of Putnamian externalism.[11] Although fascinated by the implications of Putnam's Twin Earth scenario, and a staunch advocate of Putnam's externalist outlook, McCulloch nevertheless argues that we should revise certain aspects of Putnam's classical account.

According to McCulloch, there is something of a tension between the two parts of Putnam's externalist position. The second part of Putnam's claim – the part about the dependence of meaning on the (local) environment – is construed by McCulloch as "the doctrine that *the understanding tracks real essence*" (McCulloch 1995, p. 163). We can easily appreciate why McCulloch puts the point in those terms. Consider, for example, what we just said about "water". What we mean by "water" is, paradigmatically, the stuff in earthly lakes and oceans. We don't give up talking about "water", however, no matter what discoveries about the microstructure of this stuff that we make. If we *did* give up talking about "water", say, if we found out that the stuff wasn't really colorless, or if it did not have the chemical structure we used to think it had, then this would show that our understanding of "water" was tied very intimately to an "operational definition" (in terms of chemical structure, etc.). As it is, however, our understanding of "water" is *not* tied in this way to such a definition, but rather follows or "tracks" the "essence" of this local stuff, *whatever that essence might be*. What we mean by water is *this* stuff; whatever its hidden, perhaps forever hidden, *real* essence (as supposed to what we might at this or that point in time *think* the essence of water is) might be – our understanding "tracks" it.

This first part of Putnam's claim, according to McCulloch, does not sit well with the second part. I am not certain that McCulloch wants to deny that a linguistic community has any role whatsoever in fixing meaning; rather, the problem is that the introduction of the community clouds what McCulloch thinks is the central point in Putnam's argument, namely the point that "understanding tracks real essence". For the existence of experts who can distinguish samples of a substance from superficially similar things is elsewhere said by Putnam not to be necessary for the understanding's tracking of real essence. As he puts it, "the extension of the term 'water' was just as much H_2O on Earth in 1750 [when no one knew this] as in 1950" (MM: 224). Indeed, it is not clear that this point requires even the *existence* of other speakers: on the face of it, it is just a claim about an individual's understanding tracking the unknown facts about real essence (McCulloch 1995, p. 178).

In fact, in a section appropriately entitled "Let's Be Realistic", Putnam divorces the *Bedeutung* (the "real essence") of "gold" from our ability to discover it "even *in principle*" (Putnam 1975, p. 238). So if Putnam is willing to go that far – if, that is, my understanding of "water", "gold", etc. tracks real essence *no matter whether I or anyone else are even in principle able to discover this real essence* – then why does he need the reference to expert speakers? Indeed, why the reference to anyone else at all? Is it not just a question of "an individual's understanding tracking the unknown facts about real essence"? Putnam's discussion of these issues in fact illustrates a quite different point than the one intended, according to McCulloch, namely the point "that speakers can get hold of words they do not really understand" (McCulloch 1995, p. 178). For the discussion shows that Putnam simply does not understand the words "beech" and "elm" – that they are "pretty meaningless *to him*" (ibid., p. 179). One might worry that McCulloch makes "understanding a word" into too much of an "all or nothing" affair. Putnam, it seems, certainly has *some* understanding of "beech" and "elm"; there are, in fact, quite a number of moves in language-games that Putnam would be able to make with these words, given his "concept" of them (for instance, he could correct people who think "elm" is the name of a species of coniferous tree). If this sort of vague or (very) imperfect understanding were not allowed to count as some sort of understanding, wouldn't we have to say that most words are "pretty meaningless" to most of us?[12]

Yet this is not the crucial point here. The crucial point, for McCulloch and for us, is that if Putnam's claim is that our "understanding tracks real essence" no matter whether we will ever be able to discover the real essence in question, then the reference to the existence of expert speakers, or even to other speakers as such is completely unnecessary. When Putnam *does* refer to such things it gives the impression that he is arguing for a quite different type of externalism, namely one that denies that "the mind is self-contained *with respect to the doings of other speakers*" (McCulloch 1995, p. 180). But this is dangerously misleading. For the latter kind of externalism is compatible with the denial of the

Putnamian insight that McCulloch thinks is crucial, in that "[t]his time there is nothing like a real essence which the understanding is said to track" (ibid.).

By now the motivation for McCulloch's critique of Putnam should begin to become clear to us. McCulloch is concerned to use the Twin Earth fiction to argue for what he calls "a very strong form of in-the-world Wittgensteinianism" (McCulloch 1995, p. 181). In-the-world Wittgensteinianism will

> make essential mention of aspects of the individual's surroundings, and the more inclusive and specific these descriptions are allowed to be, and the more they mention comparatively remote aspects of the world [...], the more extreme will be our form of in-the-world Wittgensteinianism [...] (McCulloch 1995, p. 99)

So the "strength" of McCulloch's version of the view has a lot to do with an emphasis on realism already implicit in his talk of "unknown facts about real essence", and clearly discernible in his dissatisfaction with Putnam's emphasis on the linguistic community. We have not learned the lesson McCulloch wants us to learn from Putnam's fiction if we do not see it in the light of "realism, the view that things can have their own nature which goes beyond how they impinge on us" (McCulloch 1995, p. 174). We "must be prepared to admit that something could, possibly, impinge on our awareness in normal conditions in exactly the same way as water yet still fail to be water" (ibid.). In fact, McCulloch seems to imply that there is no limit to the "remoteness" of the aspects of the world that will be mentioned in McCulloch's in-the-world Wittgensteinianism. After all, when McCulloch unhesitatingly describes his version of "in-the-world Wittgensteinianism" as *very* strong (cf. McCulloch 1995, p. 181), what could make it *very* strong if not precisely the metaphysical realist assumption that our understanding "tracks real essence" regardless of whether or not it is even *in principle* inaccessible to us?[13]

But what has this to do with Wittgenstein? McCulloch thinks his realistic externalism can be reconciled with Wittgenstein if we construe "'use', 'form of life', and so on [so] that they too track real essence" (McCulloch 1995, p. 181). According to this interpretation, to understand the word "water" is ultimately "to participate in certain forms of life which themselves, besides of course involving bodily and other factors, track the differences between e.g. H₂O and XYZ, even when these are unknown to the speakers" (McCulloch 1995, p. 188).

The question that I will attempt to raise in the following two sections is the extent to which McCulloch's strong "in-the-world Wittgensteinianism" can be spoken of as a form of Wittgensteinianism at all. To put it differently, I want to question whether the very realistic form of externalism that emerges in McCulloch's critical discussion of Putnam is a form of externalism that Wittgenstein might subscribe to. I will take my point of departure in a quite simple consideration of Wittgenstein's so-called "private language argument".[14]

IV. The Private Language Argument

There are, I think, several different arguments that can be distinguished in Wittgenstein's discussions of private language. These strands of argumentation are closely connected, but for the present discussion of externalism it is useful to distinguish between three more or less different motifs. Each of these will prove important to the discussion of "Wittgensteinian" externalism. In the present section, I will briefly present these three arguments, before launching my critique of McCulloch in the following section.

(a) It takes Two

If one were to sum up a central feature of Wittgenstein's private language argument, one might perhaps, inspired by a famous remark by Austin, say that it is this: it takes (at least) two to make (linguistic) meaning. However, as is painfully evident to anyone who has just a superficial acquaintance with the literature on Wittgenstein, it is much debated in which way, exactly, it "takes two" to make meaning. Does it mean that there is no hope for a wolf-child, a neonate Crusoe? Does it mean, in other words, that, given the actual absence of other persons, a person would be unable to construct a language for herself? Or does it mean, rather, that it is impossible to construct a language that is private in the sense that others, if there were any, *could not possibly* understand it or learn to understand it? In other words, that our Crusoe would very well be able to construct a language for himself, only not one that others, if he should happen to meet any, were in principle barred from ever learning to understand. And what about the external, non-human, environment? Would a wolf-child be able to construct a language given a suitable "object-environment"? Or, again, is some contribution from others what is needed, either alone or in conjunction with such an object-environment?

If these questions were easily given conclusive answers, the debate about Wittgenstein's thoughts on a "private language" would have faded out a long time ago. But the debate seems alive and well. Crucial in the debate has been the correct interpretation of Wittgenstein's remarks on rule following: The question, to put it in very general terms, has been what sort of "practice" it is that is supposed to ensure that there *is* such a thing as following a rule. In section 202 of the *Investigations,* Wittgenstein writes:

> And hence also 'obeying a rule' is a practice. And to *think* one is obeying a rule is not to obey a rule. Hence it is not possibly to obey a rule 'privately': otherwise thinking one was obeying a rule would be the same thing as obeying it.

But is he necessarily referring to a *social* practice, or could it be a "solitary" practice? That is the moot point, and the passage does not seem to settle the issue. Other passages are equally inconclusive: "Is what we call 'obeying a rule' something that it would be possible for only *one* man to do, and to do only *once* in his life? [...] It is not possible that there should have been only one occasion on which someone obeyed a rule" (Wittgenstein 1963, § 199). Is it the "once" or the "one person" (*nur ein Mensch*), which is important here? The emphasis might seem to be on the first option,[15] but both in § 199 of the *Investigations*, and again in the *Remarks on the Foundation of Mathematics* (Part VI, § 32) – Wittgenstein speaks of rule following as an "institution", which seems to imply a community of speakers. In this paper, I will more or less sidestep these questions. What is of interest to me in this part of the private language discussion is something that most if not all sides in the debate *agree on*. Let me briefly indicate what that is.

One of the first to articulate the view that a community is needed to make linguistic meaning was Saul Kripke in his 1982 book *Wittgenstein on Rules and Private Language*. Based on a detailed and by now almost classical (but widely repudiated) account of Wittgenstein's rule-following considerations Kripke argued that Wittgenstein's private language argument was leveled against the idea that "the notion of a person following a given rule is to be analyzed simply in terms of facts about the rule follower and the rule follower alone, without reference to his membership in a wider community" (Kripke 1982, p. 109). Kripke's basic claim is that an individual can only be said to grasp a concept (Kripke focuses on that of addition) if his or her uses of it "agree with those of the community in enough cases, especially the simple ones" (Kripke 1982, p. 92). Without the possibility of checking one's individual use against an established community use there can be no rule following and hence no language. Some recent commentators, among others Savigny (1996, pp. 94-125) and Williams (1999), have seconded the Kripkean emphasis on community. In Williams' formulation of the view, Wittgenstein is emphasizing the normativity of rules: "It is only in relation to the structured practice of the community that the individual can engage in normative activity" (Williams 1999, p. 187), and since language essentially is such an activity, it cannot be an individual affair (cf. ibid., p. 157).

From early on, however, the "community reading" has been challenged. Some of the fiercest opponents of the view are G. P. Baker and P. M. S. Hacker.[16] A standard objection to the community interpretation is that it is not the encouraging and corrective responses from other subjects that function as the necessary stabilizers for language, but rather the individual's environment: "reality must be sufficiently stable so that the yardstick typically gives the same result when the same object is measured on successive occasions. Otherwise measurement in particular and the application of concepts to reality in general become pointless" (Baker and Hacker 1984, p. 44; cf. 1985, p. 179). To see this, one should consider Wittgenstein's much quoted example about the putative private speaker keeping track of his sensations (Wittgenstein 1963, §§ 258-261). When a particular sensation appears, he gives it the name "S", writes it in his diary, etc. But the next time the private linguist writes "S" – how can he know that it is the same sensation again? An answer is ready to hand: He remembers the sensation he had the last time, of course, and recognizes that it is there again. But the point is that the memory of the private linguist must play a role here that is very different from the role memory usually plays in our lives. The problem is not that the private linguist might have a faulty memory of the sensation he called "S", but in a sense the opposite: *there can in principle be no such thing as misremembering,* since whatever *seems* right to the private linguist *is* right. Normally we would be able to check our memory against others, and against the objects in our environment. But there is no such thing for the private linguist. There can be no independent criteria of success and failure. He is like a solitary marksman on a shooting range who is in principle able only to see the target down the sight of his rifle right before he fires and never again.[17] Here, target practice obviously becomes senseless. In the same way rule following (and hence language) becomes meaningless when "*there is nothing independent* to which to appeal" (Hacker 1997, p. 269). But the appeal, here, only needs to be to something independent; it does not need to be an appeal to the practice of a linguistic community.[18]

Finally, there are some commentators who do not fit perfectly into either the community camp or the Baker/Hacker camp. David Pears has argued extensively for something that closely resembles the Baker/Hacker view, but at the same time is somewhat less dismissive of the community view. According to Pears, Wittgenstein had both community and environment in mind as stabilizing factors, and he would probably have refused "to choose a precise point on the line of escalating deprivations resulting from the solipsist's retreat into his microcosm, and to claim that it is just here that language becomes impossible" (Pears 1988, p. 364). Nevertheless, Pears thinks there is a certain hierarchy between the two stabilizers:

> The appeal to the community is not final, because factual language, whether spoken by a solitary person or by millions, has to preserve the constancy required if yesterday's predictions are to come true today. The individual gets confirmation from the community only on the assumption that the community's usage has itself remained constant. (Pears 1988, p. 369)

In other words, individual language usage might be answerable to the community, but the community's language usage (as well as the individual's) "is answerable to the world" (ibid.). Both factors are important, but in the end the right kind of physical environment is a more important stabilizer than the social environment.

To sum up, it seems fair to say that there are (at least) three general takes on this first aspect of Wittgenstein's critique of "private language": Some emphasize the necessity of a stabilizing social community; others emphasize the necessity of a stabilizing object-environment; and others again argue that while Wittgenstein sets no precise limit specifying where linguistic meaning becomes impossible, he would hold that if there were not a stabilizing factor – either in the shape of a community or in the shape of a stable object-environment – then language definitely would be impossible. If one of these interpretations is correct, then the immediate consequence of Wittgenstein's "private language argument" is that he must be committed to *some* form of externalism. Linguistic meaning cannot, it seems, be generated "internally" in a subject, without essential reference to the subject's environment. This is something *all* the mentioned commentators seem to agree on. In some sense, meaning is co-determined by external factors: a stable world and/or community. Or, to speak the language of Putnam, knowing the meaning of a term is not "just a matter of being in a certain psychological state", where "being in a psychological state" is understood as something that does not presuppose "the existence of any individual other than the subject to whom that state is ascribed" (Putnam 1975, pp. 219-20). Grasping a meaning is something that cannot take place outside some rule-governed practice; and no practice can be rule-governed unless there is *something* outside the individual subject, and unless this "something" is in a certain way. On all accounts of Wittgenstein's private language argument that I have sketched in the subsection, meaning, to use a phrase from Putnam, is *interactional* (cf. Putnam 1988, p. 36). That is, meanings, according to Wittgenstein, too, simply "ain't in the *head*" (Putnam 1975, p. 227). We should also note that the private language discussion is structurally parallel to Putnam's and McCulloch's discussion. A crucial issue is how to place the external emphasis, so to speak: on the world or on the community. But all agree that the upshot of the private language considerations is some such external emphasis.[19]

(b) Stage-setting

At one point in his story of the solitary diarist, Wittgenstein interrupts the discussion of lack of criteria for rightness and wrongness with a somewhat different consideration: "What reason have we for calling 'S' the sign for a *sensation*? For 'sensation' is a word of our common language, not of one intelligible to me alone" (Wittgenstein 1963, § 261). The point is not merely that "sensation" happens to be a word that is not private in the required sense. The point is rather that by speaking of "sensation", the would-be private linguist draws upon the full-fledged public language in a very substantial way. Wittgenstein had already introduced this claim four sections earlier:

> When one says "He gave a name to his sensation" one forgets that a great deal of stage-setting in the language is presupposed if the mere act of naming is to make sense. And when we speak of someone's having given a name to pain, what is presupposed is the existence of the grammar of the word "pain"; it shews the post where the new word is stationed. (ibid., § 257)

A number of commentators have emphasized the importance of this aspect of the private language argument.[20] What Wittgenstein is trying to show, they convincingly argue, is that if the private linguist stipulates that "S" is the name of a *sensation*, then she has helped herself to a crucial category of our normal, public language. "Sensation" makes sense only in contrast to other categories, such as "thought", "emotion", and even words for physical things, states, and processes. When our private linguist says that "S" is the name of a *sensation*, she is, as Wittgenstein points out, indicating the "post" on which this new name is to be placed. But thereby the private linguist tacitly invokes the *stage-setting* provided by our public language. That is, she does not "enter the world of a private language semantically naked", as Robert Fogelin has put it (Fogelin 1976, p. 161). And if that is so, then her language is not all that private after all: it draws on a public language, which among other things contains words referring to things outside the individual speaker.

A tempting move to make for the would-be private linguist, then, is to give up the category of "sensation": at least when she writes "S", she "has *something*" (Wittgenstein 1963, § 261), it might be insisted. Surely, there is "something there"; she "has" ("senses", but we are not allowed to say that) something, and why can't she simply name this *something* "S" ("*This* is 'S'")?[21] Here Wittgenstein launches a second wave of attacks. First, he points out that the words "has" and "something" also belong to our public language (Wittgenstein 1963, § 261). So when using these, the private linguist is still not linguistically naked enough, so to speak. Secondly, supposing that the private linguist could avoid the first difficulty somehow, what she must do then is to perform some private or inner act of ostension. But how is that supposed to work? To put it differently, what is the "*this*" that is being named? Take the example of a "normal" ostensive definition. I point to a big Labrador and tell my little nephew, "This is p". How can this be of any use to someone who does not even have an idea of the category of "p", that is, someone who does not yet know "the overall role of the word in language" (Wittgenstein 1963, § 30) (are we talking about a color, an animal, etc.)? After all, "p" could be filled in with many different words ("black"; "big"; "a carnivore", "a dog"; "something with four legs"; "Rover") (cf. ibid., § 28), and just a little reflection tells us that there is not, in general, any difference in the *way we point* when we are trying to define a color, rather than a species of animal. So, assuming that the framework is still lacking, and that we thus do not know at which "post" to place the word "p", it is entirely unclear what has been defined. That is to say, *nothing* (in particular) has been defined. So, to return to our would-be private linguist, what does she accomplish by concentrating her attention on whatever it is that she has? If she has *no framework* in place, what could it possibly mean for her to be defining one thing rather than another (this *type* of sensation; this level of *intensity*; this *particular* sensation; and so forth)?[22] Note, by the way, that this discussion, too, has broadly externalist implications. The argument seems in part to rely on the assumption that the private language cannot be set up "from scratch", that it needs the framework of our public language to get off the ground. And this framework contains references to other people and to the "external" world. Wittgenstein's point, once again, is that linguistic meaning cannot merely be a question of what goes on inside an individual.

One may reach the same point from a different angle. My inner act of concentration, one could say, does not fix any *technique for using the word* "S". What Wittgenstein writes in another context concerning "normal" ostension also holds for "private" ostension:

> One can say: Whoever has a word explained by reference to a patch of colour only knows *what* is meant to the extent that he knows *how* the word is to be used. That is to say: there is no grasping or understanding of the object, except by the grasping of a technique.[23] (Wittgenstein 1980b, § 296; cf. 1963, § 199)

To speak a language, as already mentioned above, is to partake in a practice rooted in our lives. Even though ostensive definitions play some role in our lives, they cannot play the role the private linguist needs them to play. For what is "S" to be used *for*; what is its *function*? When and how is it appropriate to use "S", what is the appropriate "technique"? The private linguist would presumably say that "S" is used to signify something (namely *this*), but this in fact says nothing about the *use* of the word (cf. Wittgenstein 1980a, § 614). "Signifying" is everything and nothing (just as "this" is everything and nothing), and thus it remains as unclear as before how "S" is supposed to connect up with our lives, how it fits into our practices and how we are to use it. Clearly, this connects back to our previous discussion in (a), for to speak of "practices" and "techniques" is of course to invoke normativity and criteria for right and wrong performance. So, to bring the subsection's point in contact with the point of the previous subsection, the private inner act of ostension takes place in a complete conceptual and practical vacuum, so to speak: there is no conceptual and practical framework into which it might be fitted, and there are no independent criteria of success and failure.

(c) Wheels Turning Idly
In his influential review of the *Philosophical Investigations* Norman Malcolm distinguishes between an "internal" and an "external" private language argument in Wittgenstein's magnum opus. The "internal" argument roughly corresponds to what has already been said above in (a) and (b). Whether the decisive lacking stabilizers are interpreted as having their origin in the community or in the world, the "internal" argument has the same form, namely that of a *re-*

ductio ad absurdum: "postulate a 'private' language; then deduce that it is not *language*" (Malcolm 1966, p. 75). The external argument proceeds in a slightly different way. Here the emphasis is not on the lack of stabilizers or restrictions necessary for establishing and maintaining meaning, nor on the stage-setting without which ostensive definition cannot get off the ground, but rather on the *public import* of private objects, assuming they could be privately dubbed (which the "internal" arguments have said they could not).[24] The crucial passage in the external argument is the famous parable about beetles in boxes:

> Now someone tells me that *he* knows what pain is only from his own case! – Suppose everyone had a box with something in it: we call it a "beetle". No one can look into anyone else's box, and everyone says he knows what a beetle is only by looking at *his* beetle. – Here it would be quite possible for everyone to have something different in his box. One might even imagine such a thing constantly changing. – But suppose the word "beetle" had a use in these people's language? – If so it would not be used as the name of a thing. The thing in the box has no place in the language-game at all; not even as a *something*: for the box might even be empty. – No, one can 'divide through' by the thing in the box; it cancels out, whatever it is.
>   That is to say: if we construe the grammar of the expression of sensation on the model of "object and designation" the object drops out of consideration as irrelevant (Wittgenstein 1963, § 293).

The point of this passage is not to show that the feeling of pain, its subjective qualitative character, is "irrelevant" to the meaning of the word "pain".[25] The point is rather that *if* we construe this "feeling of pain" in a particular way, *then* it becomes irrelevant; and that, since this conclusion is absurd, we should deny the particular conception of pain that leads to the conclusion. That is, Wittgenstein is again putting forward a *reductio*. The problematic assumption is of course the one that makes "pain" look like a "beetle in a box". *If* the sensation of pain is really something *essentially cut off from public life*; if it is something each of us knows about, identifies, and names, only from his or her own case; *then* it follows, Wittgenstein claims, that the sensation is irrelevant to our use of "pain"-words. The "thing in the box", one might say, is a wheel turning idly (cf. Wittgenstein 1963, § 271), since "it does not connect with the use (i.e. the meaning) of the word" (McGinn 1997, p. 173). The use of the word, the public practice, cannot revolve around an object that *per definition cannot make a difference to public life*.

But is this really convincing? Does it not just show that Wittgenstein's private language argument is "no more than a verificationist defense of logical behaviorism" (cf. McGinn 1997, p. 130)?[26] I think it does not. One point that bears emphatic repetition here is that in Wittgenstein's parable "pain" is conceived of as completely cut off from public life and the "external world": *all ties have been severed* (this is one reason why the image of the beetle as being "in a box" is so appropriate: it depicts the beetle as cut off from the world by the sides of the box, as it were).[27] What Wittgenstein is sketching here, in other words, has a lot to do with what McCulloch describes as the idea that "the mind is self-contained" with respect to the social and material world (McCulloch 1995, p. 47; cf. p. 109). This self-containedness thesis is ultimately a quite radical thesis (for one thing, it certainly implies a very strong form of internalism), and one should not jump to the conclusion that everyone who denies it is *eo ipso* a behaviorist. McCulloch has shown this very convincingly, emphasizing the crucial difference between behaviorism and *behavior-embracing mentalism* (McCulloch 2003, pp. 12-13 and passim).[28] Wittgenstein's beetle parable is designed to show the inadequacy of behavior-*rejecting* mentalism, to use McCulloch's vocabulary – Wittgenstein tries to show that such a position tends, strangely enough, to lead to a variant of behaviorism – and his agenda is to endorse behavior-embracing mentalism, not behaviorism.

Thus, if there *were* essentially private "things" of the "beetle" sort, and if these *could* be dubbed "beetles" by each individual, privately, then these things would, in the public language that we actually speak, be nothing but wheels turning idly. They would have no function or place whatsoever. Again, then, we seem to be driven towards an externalist position: what *I* mean by the word "beetle", given a language shared with others, is not just a question of what goes on inside me. In fact, if what goes on "inside me" were *completely severed* from the public world, it would be completely irrelevant to my use of the word, according to Wittgenstein (cf. Wittgenstein 1958, pp. 72-73).[29] In this connection, we should also note the well-known fact that Wittgenstein repeatedly connects meaning with "use". It is, of course, controversial, what exactly should be concluded from his famous remark that "For a *large* class of cases – though not for all – in which we employ the word 'meaning' it can be defined thus: the meaning of a word is its use in the language" (Wittgenstein 1963, § 43; cf. §§ 421, 532, p. 220).[30] But at least it does associate the meaning of some words with the use made of them in language. More important to our present concerns is the fact that Wittgenstein occasionally contrasts the "use" or "application" made of a word with what goes on inside the individual speaker. Later in the *Philosophical Investigations* he thus emphasizes that what I *mean* is a question of the "use" I make of words, rather than what goes on "in my mind". As he puts it, "What is essential is to see that the same thing can come before our minds when we hear the word and the application still be different. Has it the *same* meaning both times? I think we shall say not" (Wittgenstein 1963, § 140). I take it that this remark implies that two speakers could be "psychologically indistinguishable" (in Putnam's sense), while the "application" and hence the *meanings* of their words were nevertheless different. If so, it clearly illustrates Wittgenstein's commitment to *some* form of semantic externalism.

So, to sum up the results of this section, there is an externalism in Wittgenstein's private language argument in the following sense: *understanding the meaning of a word (sentence, etc.) is not merely a question of what goes on inside an individual, independently of the nature of this individual's (physical and social) environment*. Clearly, this is not without further ado to be identified with Putnam and McCulloch's specific versions of externalism. For one thing, their discussions focus on content and reference, whereas Wittgenstein's private language argument mainly seems to be concerned with the question of the "conditions for the possibility" of linguistic meaning as such, if one may put it in such Kantian terms.[31] Yet Wittgenstein's reflections on private language do have important consequences for content externalism. This will be the subject of the following section.

V. Wittgensteinian Externalism and "Tracking Real Essence"

As already mentioned, McCulloch intends to make his "in-the-world Wittgensteinianism" fit the realism that he distills from Putnam's Twin Earth fantasy by construing "'use', 'form of life', and so on [so] that they too track real essence" (McCulloch 1995, p. 181). But will that work? Can one interpret Wittgenstein in this way without *mis*construing his position? The issue is not whether McCulloch is right to attribute a general externalist outlook to Wittgenstein – we have seen that this is correct – but whether Wittgenstein's externalism can be of the same *type* as McCulloch's externalism.

Anthony Rudd has recently argued that McCulloch's Putnamian externalism cannot be made to harmonize with a Wittgensteinian externalism. According to Rudd, Wittgenstein's externalism can be formulated in the following way:

> Understanding is something that is manifested in practice, in using words appropriately in contexts. So the understanding cannot be said to exist apart from the contexts in which the

word is used. This is what the slogan "Meaning is use" (*PI* §43) comes down to. It is not a theory about what meaning essentially is; it is a reminder to us of the ways in which we ascribe mastery of a concept to a person. (Rudd 1997, p. 501; cf. 2003, p. 77)

As Rudd goes on to argue, this is hard to reconcile with McCulloch's "tracking real essence". McCulloch emphasizes the contrast between the possibly unknown and unknowable real essence that our words "track" and the "way things impinge on us", but "if understanding must be manifestable in practice, how could we manifest our grasp of what is supposed to be the reality of things in themselves, *as opposed to the way they might impinge on us*?" (Rudd 1997, p. 506; 2003, p. 83). Rudd continues his attack on McCulloch's use of Wittgenstein by emphasizing that even if we could make sense of such a grasp of the "real essence" being manifested, it is hard to see why we would be interested in this unknowable "real essence" in the first place. According to Rudd, what we ought to say, on Wittgensteinian grounds, is rather this: "If the stuff is to play some role in our form of life (if it does not, we would have no motive for wanting to include it in our classifications anyway) then it will do so in virtue of the ways it impinges on us" (Rudd 1997, p. 506; 2003, p. 83).

I agree with most of this.[32] Nevertheless, Rudd's central premise is somewhat misleading, I think. The problem is this: Rudd links his description of understanding as something that is manifested in practice with "the ways in which we ascribe mastery of a concept to a person". The emphasis is thus on third person ascriptions of understanding; in order for an individual to truly *understand* a word, she must be able in practice to demonstrate her understanding to others. This is problematic, and for two closely connected reasons.

First, it might seem to rely on a very robust community interpretation of understanding. That is, one might take Rudd to imply that understanding is essentially something a community ascribes to an individual. There can thus be no understanding for a neonate Crusoe. But as we have seen, the claim that Wittgenstein subscribes to this view is certainly contested in the literature. It therefore seems odd to presuppose this claim in an argument designed to show that McCulloch's position cannot be defended on Wittgensteinian grounds. McCulloch could surely argue that Rudd precisely misconstrues these "Wittgensteinian grounds". Understanding, of course, cannot be said to exist apart from the contexts in which words are used. But that is not in itself an argument against the idea that understanding "tracks real essence". Such an argument is only mounted once we assume with Rudd that "use" essentially refers to "manifestation in practice", which in turn refers to other speakers who, on the basis of the right kind of manifestation in the right contexts, "ascribe mastery of a concept" to the individual person. But what this comes down to is the community interpretation of private language, and this interpretation is very controversial. Nothing prevents McCulloch from rejecting it – in fact, his critical remarks on Putnam's reference to the linguistic community suggest that McCulloch would precisely reject this interpretation.[33]

Secondly, Rudd's description of understanding almost gives the impression that it can be adequately accounted for in purely behaviorist terms. When Rudd connects the "practice" and "use" of understanding with its manifestation to others, it seems to follow that understanding is simply a matter of displaying the right third person observable behavior under the right circumstances. If so, then Marie McGinn's worry that Wittgenstein is presented as formulating "a verificationist defense of logical behaviorism" (cf. McGinn 1997, p. 130) would be justified. Rudd correctly contests the behaviorist interpretation of Wittgenstein (e.g., Rudd 2003, p. 106), but one might wonder whether he should not then have couched his argument against McCulloch less exclusively in third person, observational terms.[34]

This is one reason why our discussion of Wittgenstein's private language argument is important: the private language argument precisely investigates the possibility of an individual subject grasping words *in complete isolation*. That is, it (or at least part of it) investigates this possibility from the *inside*, from a first person point of view (see, e.g., Wittgenstein 1978, Part VI, § 32). The question is whether *I* could understand words and sentences completely independently of the nature of my external (social and physical) environment. But the discussion of the private language argument is important in another way as well, in that it allows us to see quite clearly why Rudd is, after all, right to claim that McCulloch's externalism is irreconcilable with Wittgenstein's. Let me try to explain this.

When Wittgenstein emphasizes the importance of a stabilizing environment he cannot possibly mean "the real essence" of the environment as opposed to how things "impinge on us". On the contrary, meaning is *interactional*, which means that part of what is important here is precisely how the social and physical environment impinges on the individual. Wittgenstein thus gives as examples of such stabilizing factors the approval and disapproval, expectation and encouragement, that others express to us (Wittgenstein 1963, § 208); and what matters here is surely how these expressions influence us. In contrast, the hidden reality of things, precisely insofar as it is hidden, insofar as it doesn't impinge on the individual, seems irrelevant. It surely cannot function as any kind of stabilizing framework if it is in principle beyond the cognitive reach of human beings. What must provide stability for the individual speaker is her *experienced* physical and social environment.

Recall also the point that linguistic understanding is something that presupposes a practice. It seems hard to conceive of a practice (whether individual or social; whether manifested in behavior or not) that is concerned with real essences in themselves *as opposed to any way they might impinge on us*. This, I think, is Rudd's main point. We can easily conceive of practices that are concerned with the real nature of things – just think of natural science – but what are we to make of the idea of a *human practice* concerned with the *fundamentally inaccessible* nature of things? And if we cannot make sense of such a practice, what sense can we make of the suggestion that our understanding "tracks" these inaccessible real essences? Or if understanding, as Wittgenstein also emphasizes, is essentially mastering a *technique*, how do we learn to master the technique of referring to the *Ding an sich in contrast to* the thing as it could ever appear to us? It seems hard, in particular on Wittgensteinian grounds, to make sense of any of this. For Wittgenstein, the reach of our understanding seems much too closely connected with our performances and the kinds of explanations, demonstrations, and examples that we can actually give, to fit McCulloch's idea of tracking unknown and unknowable essences. To give one concrete example, the idea that our understanding tracks real essence far beyond what it is within our cognitive capacities to realize seems hard to square with Wittgenstein's hesitation as to whether we fully understand the question whether "7777" occurs in the development of π (Wittgenstein 1963, § 516).

The "beetle in the box" parable makes the incompatibility of Wittgenstein's private language argument and McCulloch's type of externalism explicit. The gist of this strand of the argument is this: that which cannot connect in any way with human social life – that is, that which cannot possibly make any difference in human social life – cannot be relevant to the "use" we make of words in our common language. It is a wheel turning idly – no part of the machinery, and thus no part of the "meaning" either. But when McCulloch contrast the ways things impinge on us and the "real essence" of these things, does he not move dangerously close to ascribing to this "real essence" precisely the role of a wheel turning idly, or a beetle that we can "divide through by"? In fact, has he not already taken this step explicitly? He seems – if I have interpreted his "very strong form of in-the-world Wittgensteinianism" correctly – to claim that our concepts (at least natural kind terms) track the real essences of things, *even if these are in principle unknown to us*. But if they never make any difference to our lives, indeed if they *cannot possibly* make any difference to our lives, then they simply reduce to beetles in boxes. On Wittgenstein's view, as we have seen, a difference that makes no difference cannot matter to the meaning of our words. Consider this passage from *The Blue Book*:

> I want to play chess, and a man gives the white king a paper crown, leaving the use of the piece unaltered, but telling me that the crown has a meaning to him in the game, which he can't express by rules. I say: "as long as it doesn't alter the use of the piece, it hasn't what I call a meaning". (Wittgenstein 1958, p. 65)

Wittgenstein' reply, then, to the claim even that part of what I mean when I say "water" is something in principle beyond the cognitive reach of a possible community would surely be that "a nothing would serve just as well" (Wittgenstein 1963, § 304) as this kind of "something".

In a sense, perhaps, Wittgenstein is too much of a pragmatist to agree with McCulloch's metaphysical realism. Wittgenstein denies being a pragmatist, but what he rejects is the suggestion that "true" equals "useful". He continues, immediately after that: "The usefulness, i.e. the use, gives the proposition its special sense, the language-game gives it" (Wittgenstein 1980a, § 266). On Wittgenstein's view, use hangs closely together with usefulness – rules and language-games have *points*! (Wittgenstein 1963, § 564) – rather than with the (possibly hidden) "reality" of things in themselves. Wittgenstein writes, "the proposition 'The Earth has existed for millions of years' makes clearer sense than the proposition 'The Earth has existed in the last five minutes'" (Wittgenstein 1963, p. 221). But why is this so? If use did "track real essence", if this was the business of language, then why would this sentence not have a clear meaning, why would it not be simply undoubtedly *true*? The answer is that language "stands in the midst of our lives" (cf. Wittgenstein 1992, p. 72), that language use is embedded in a network of human practices. It does not as it were jump out of these practices in order to track down beetles in boxes. So the proposition, "The Earth has existed in the last five minutes" has an unclear sense because it is unclear what the point of it might be. The reality of the matter it claims something about is perfectly clear, but it is entirely unclear what practice (if any) it invokes – what "game" is being played.

According to Wittgenstein, "Words have meaning only in the stream of life"

(Wittgenstein 1982, § 913). What is wrong with McCulloch's interpretation of Wittgenstein is ultimately that it moves the meaning of our words beyond our lives. (Or, alternatively, that it presents the human "form of life" as being of a thoroughly theoretical nature – as if it were the business of human life as such to "mirror reality".[35]) The world we live in, surely, is the world we experience and interact with – this is almost an analytical proposition. When McCulloch contrasts the real essence of things with things as they impinge on us in our experiences and activities, he locates the former outside "the stream of life", thereby – at least from a Wittgensteinian point of view – depriving it of any significance to the meaning of our language.

Let me end this section with a final reservation concerning McCulloch's use of Wittgenstein. McCulloch's notion of "tracking real essence", that is, going to the nature of things regardless of how they "impinge on us", seems to imply that our concepts are extremely strong and firm. What I mean is this: the discovery that the feline creatures that many of us keep as pets are in fact robots controlled from Mars (cf. Putnam 1975, p. 243) is not taken to imply any difficulties for out use of the word "cat". Our understanding *tracks the real (and possibly unknowable) essence of these things*, no matter what we might think about them, indeed no matter how bizarrely they might all of a sudden begin to "impinge on us". But is this really convincing? Austin, for one, was critical of the idea that we are conceptually equipped to handle every such situation. As he argues, considering an example resembling one of Putnam's:

> Suppose that I live in harmony and friendship for four years with a cat: and then it delivers a philippic. We ask ourselves, perhaps, 'Is it a real cat? or is it *not* a real cat?' 'Either it *is* or it *is not*, but we can't be sure which'. Now actually, that is not so: *neither* 'It is a real cat' *nor* 'it is not a real cat' fits the facts semantically: each is designed for other situations than this one. [...] Ordinary language breaks down in extraordinary cases. (In such cases, the cause of the breakdown is semantical.) Now no doubt an *ideal* language would *not* break down, whatever happened. In doing physics, for example, where our language is tightened up in order precisely to describe complicated and unusual cases concisely, we *prepare linguistically for the worst*. In ordinary language we do not: *words fail us*. (Austin 1979, pp. 67-68; cf. p. 88)

This does *not*, I hasten to add, imply a general skepticism regarding philosophical thought experiments.[36] Indeed, Austin himself makes use of one such thought experiment to make his point. Rather, it expresses skepticism with respect to the idea that we are always "linguistically prepared for the worst". If we bear in mind what was said above about the stabilizing factors of language, it should come as no surprise to us that Wittgenstein is in perfect agreement with Austin on this point. As he says in the *Philosophical Investigations*,

> It is only in normal cases that the use of a word is clearly prescribed; we know, are in no doubt, what to say in this or that case. The more abnormal the case, the more doubtful it becomes what we are to say – if there were for instance no characteristic expression of pain, of fear, of joy; if rule became exception and exception rule; or if both became phenomena of roughly equal frequency – this would make our normal language-games lose their point. – The procedure of putting a lump of cheese on a balance and fixing the price by the turn of the scale would lose its point if it frequently happened for such lumps to suddenly grow or shrink for no obvious reason. (Wittgenstein 1963, § 142)

According to Austin and Wittgenstein, we cannot simply assume the smooth functioning of our everyday language across possible worlds, Twin Earths, cats turning out to be robots controlled from Mars, and so forth. Yet if McCulloch is to drive home his point that such examples show how our concepts track real essence, then he *must* assume that they remain perfectly functioning, with *Sinn* and *Bedeutung* intact, even in the most extreme scenarios. His point, as noted, is precisely that our understanding tracks real essence no matter how things impinge on us. But perhaps our words "water" and "cat" only function in certain language games (say, the game of pointing to a picture of a cat when hearing the word "cat"; pointing to a picture of a robot when hearing the word "robot"; pointing to a picture of a tree when…; etc.). And if we change the circumstances in such bizarre ways as to make these language games pointless or impossible, then perhaps we simply no longer know what to do with those words. Words, then, simply fail us, as Austin says; they do *not* continue to operate smoothly in order to track the real essences of things, behind their confused appearances.

VI. Conclusion

McCulloch, I have argued, ultimately cannot make his metaphysical realist concerns harmonize with Wittgenstein. On Wittgenstein's view, our language is tied to our *lives*, rather than to mysterious essences transcending the world as it "impinges on us" in our lives. As tied to our lives, language is also essentially tied to the world; Wittgenstein is, in this sense, clearly advocating an form of "externalism". Yet the world in question is precisely the world as it impinges on our lives. Of course it is true that things could be different from how they seem to us to be; a broomstick partly immersed in water looks bent to all of us, but it *is* straight. No sane person would deny that. But to divorce the "real essence" of things completely from they way they impinge on us, or possibly could impinge on us, is quite a different matter; and Wittgenstein would reject *this* (distinctly philosophical) move.

Is this "to embrace a very forthright form of idealism", as McCulloch claims (cf. McCulloch 1995, p. 174)? Or is it rather just to embrace our natural (or common sense) realism, while refusing to follow the philosopher who insists on adding something "queer" by demanding that this natural realism "bear metaphysical weight"?[37] I think the latter is true, and that it perfectly illustrates Wittgenstein's attitude to the opposing positions of idealism and realism. As he writes in the *Philosophical Investigations*,

> *this* is what disputes between Idealists, Solipsists and Realists look like. The one party attack the normal form of expression as if they were attacking a statement; the others defend it, as if they were stating facts recognized by every reasonable human being. (Wittgenstein 1963, § 402)

Perhaps the reason why McCulloch thinks he can make our "normal form of expression" bear metaphysical weight is that he is attached to a more fundamental, distinctly un-Wittgensteinian idea. This is the idea that it is possible to occupy an "external point of view" on language and reality (cf. Crary 2000, pp. 3-4, 6),[38] that is, the idea that it is possible to provide what McDowell has called "a sideways-on picture of understanding and the world" (McDowell 1996, p. 82). It is only if it is supposed that we can step out of our lives and achieve an external view on the relation between our language and the world that the idea of our language as "tracking real essences", no matter whether we could possibly have any cognitive access to these essences, makes sense. And it is only from this standpoint that the denial of this idea must look like "a very forthright form of idealism". Because, seen from an external standpoint (if it were possible), such a denial would amount to either a rejection of the idea that our language and experience hook on to this real world at all (epistemic anti-realism), or a rejection of the idea that there is any such world apart from our linguistic and other practices (metaphysical idealism). But the whole thing is an illusion. We cannot adopt such an external viewpoint from which to compare our linguistic practices with the world they connect with. We only have access to the real world, and to the real essences of things, *in and through our lives*.[39]

Notes

1. See Searle 1983, p. 230, for an explicit defense of this view.
2. The implicit assumption about the mind is a central one in philosophy since Descartes; McCulloch calls it the view that the mind is "self-contained" with respect to the world (including at least most of the human body). I might have the thoughts, perceptions, etc. that I have *without there being any "external" world at all*.
3. But "psychological state" need not be understood as referring to a state of the (Cartesian) mind in contrast to the brain. Nor should it be understood as implying that "knowing the meaning of a word" is some continuously occurrent state. In any case, Putnam's precise way of formulating the issues is not important to the argument here, except indirectly, insofar as a certain critique of Putnam will concern us later.
4. What Putnam introduces here under the heading "psychological state properly so called" or "psychological state in the narrow sense" (Putnam 1975, p. 220) is of course what has later become known as "narrow content". Although I cannot argue the point here I agree with John McDowell that the question Putnam should have raised (but did not) in this connection is whether this "narrow" conception of psychological states should really be identified with the psychological state *properly so called*. In other words, while he criticizes an "isolationistic" conception of meaning, Putnam seems to take an "isolationistic" conception of the mind for granted. According to McDowell, what Putnam ought to have argued is that neither meaning *nor the mind* is in the head (McDowell 1998, pp. 276, 291). This is indeed also an extension to Putnam that McCulloch has argued emphatically for (see especially McCulloch 2003, pp. 41-45).
5. I follow Putnam's way of formulating the scenario here. But it has no substantial effect on the argument if we say instead that the two Hilarys are physically indistinguishable, "atom for atom" type-identical etc. (Though of course it complicates matters, since the human body contains a considerable amount of H2O.)
6. For some discussion of the potency of this argument, see Searle 1983, p. 202, and Putnam 1988, p. 29.
7. This is no longer science fiction, and the element of fiction is greatly reduced. In fact, the Dutch word *meer* means, roughly, lake, whereas the German *Meer* means, roughly, sea. Conversely, when a Dutch speaker says *zee* she means, roughly, sea, while the German *See* means, roughly, lake (such "switching" is perhaps not uncommon among closely related languages). So just suppose that we are talking about the same language ("Germanic"), with these as the only differences of dialect, and we have an almost perfect Earth equivalent of Putnam's switching example.
8. Tyler Burge (1979) argues at length for a similar point (but see his reservations regarding Putnam at pp. 117-118). Burge, incidentally, provides answers to some of the questions one might want to raise concerning Putnam's argument. First of all, one could claim that there is a crucial difference, overlooked by Putnam, between what *the word* means when uttered by me, and what *I* mean when I utter the word. Burge calls this the "argument from deviant speaker-meaning", and he argues that it downplays the important fact that a speaker is typically willing "to submit his statement and belief to the arbitration of an authority, [which] suggests a willingness to have his words taken in the normal way" (Burge 1979, p. 101). Thus, when I say "elm", I do not mean to be referring to just any big deciduous tree, even if my grasp of the word doesn't allow me to pick out elms from other deciduous trees; rather, I mean to be referring to *elms*, and if on any particular occasion others correct me when I apply the word "elm", I do not protest that they have misunderstood what *I* mean when I say "elm". Secondly, one could also claim that arguments like Putnam's and Burge's are only effective when incom-

plete understanding is involved. Burge anticipates this response and tries to show that *"even those propositional attitudes not infected by incomplete understanding* depend for their content on social factors" (Burge 1979, p. 84). Here, he relies on a reversal of his familiar arthritis argument. The argument runs roughly like this: A patient thinks (correctly) that he suffers from arthritis in some of his joints. He also thinks that arthritis is something that only occurs in joints. He now goes to see his doctor because of pains in his left thigh. Holding everything "internal" to the patient (his pains, dispositions, physical history) constant, Burge invites us to imagine the following twist to the story. When the man complains to his doctor about the new pains in his thigh, the doctor informs him that this is yet another case of arthritis. The man reacts with surprise to this bit of information, of course, but the doctor assures him that "arthritis" applies to all kinds of rheumatism; in fact she even looks it up in the dictionary just to set the patient's mind at ease. So here our patient is corrected in the same way I could be when applying the word "elm" to an oak in the presence of a botanist. That is to say, both doctor and patient in this story work with a different concept of "arthritis" than we do. Yet all we have done is to change the social surroundings of our original patient, whose understanding of (our concept of) arthritis was perfectly in order (cf. Burge 1979, p. 84).

9. Actually, Putnam thinks this is impossible, since we have *established scientifically* that water *is* H2O (cf. Putnam 1975, p. 233). But in any case, we can just change the example. Putnam himself considers the possibility that the creatures we call "cats" might in fact turn out to be robots controlled from Mars. Here, so Putnam claims, we would *not* conclude that there are no cats, but that cats are robots controlled from Mars (Putnam 1975, p. 243).

10. As Putnam concludes in another paper: "extension [...] is, in some cases, 'part of the meaning'" (Putnam 1975, p. 151). Note that Searle accepts many of Putnam's claims here, but attempts to use them to argue for the opposite, *internalist* thesis that meanings *are* in the head (Searle 1983, pp. 202-208). Searle's argument cannot be reviewed properly here. But let me point out two things about it. First, it seems to me that Searle is not really arguing against Putnam's position. Searle thus claims that Putnam's examples are insufficient to refute the "thesis that meaning determines reference" (Searle 1983, p. 201; cf. p. 206). This is a puzzling claim, since Putnam explicitly states that he wants to *hold on* to the idea that meaning determines extension (Putnam 1975, p. 270). The tie he wants to sever is the one between what is "in the head" and meaning. Perhaps the reason why Searle overlooks this is that he takes it as simply obvious that meaning (or content) is "in the head" – as he says, there is nowhere else for it to be (Searle 1983, p. 200; cf. p. 208). Secondly, it is worth emphasizing that much in Searle's argument depends on the claim that some intentional experiences (such as perceptions) are "causally self-referential". I think there is reason to be skeptical of this claim. Does it really fit the phenomenology of the matter to say that every time I perceive something (say, a yellow station car), it is part of the content of my perception that the experience is *caused* by the car? It is true, of course, that it is *not* part of the content of my experience that it is caused by *me*. But then it is not evident that any kind of causation need be part of the content of the experience at all, and as a matter of fact I think it usually is not. (See also the penultimate note to this paper.)

11. McCulloch continues the discussion of Twin Earth and his defense of externalism in his last book, *The Life of the Mind* (2003). But the critical discussion of Putnam, and the claim that McCulloch's own position is a "Wittgensteinianism", are unfolded in the earlier book. My discussion will therefore focus on the latter.

12. Burge (1979) argues convincingly that "incomplete understanding" is much more widespread than philosophers have often assumed. Recall also that Burge's reversed arthritis argument showed that social dependency holds also where no incomplete understanding is involved.

13. Putnam, remember, explicitly took this step (cf. Putnam 1975, p. 238); and when McCulloch comments on this he expresses no reservations. In fact, he seems to think the idealistic alternative is so unconvincing that it isn't even necessary to argue for Putnam's realistic position. He brushes the whole issue aside with the remark: "If you like, consider Putnam's argument to be qualified with an initial 'If realism is correct, then...'" (McCulloch 1995, p. 174).
14. I write "so-called" because of the familiar claim that Wittgenstein does not present any such *argument*. This claim is typically part of a more general claim concerning Wittgenstein's approach to philosophy, stressing the descriptive and (especially) "therapeutic" nature of Wittgenstein's philosophy and repudiating the idea that Wittgenstein aims to provide any "positive" philosophy at all. In the following discussion I shall omit the "so-called" for stylistic reasons. But my discussion should be read as non-committal with regard to the questions of whether Wittgenstein's thoughts on private language constitute an "argument" (implies "theses"), whether Wittgenstein provides any "theory of (linguistic) meaning" (e.g., "meaning is use"), and so forth. My point is a much more modest one. An additional reason for saying "so-called" private language argument, by the way, is that I think there are several different lines of argumentation that Wittgenstein pursues.
15. In his answer to the question, Wittgenstein does not respond to the point about a single person, but only to the point about a single occasion. And in the *Remarks on the Foundation of Mathematics*, Part VI, § 21, which contains similar remarks, Wittgenstein does not refer to the idea of a single person following a rule at all. How this should be interpreted is itself disputed, of course. Maybe Wittgenstein thinks it too obvious that an isolated individual cannot follow a rule to even deserve mention. But then why does he think it worth posing the question in the *Investigations*? See also Wittgenstein 1978, Part VI, § 34: "In order to describe the phenomenon of language, one must describe a practice, not something that happens once, *no matter of what kind*".
16. But they are far from alone. See Kenny 1975, chapter 10, Budd 1989, chapters 2 and 3, and McGinn 1984, chapter 2, for examples of equally fierce opposition to the community interpretation.
17. I borrow this illuminating example from David Pears (Pears 1988, pp. 333, 395). Wittgenstein's own example is that of someone who buys several copies of the same newspaper to assure himself of the truth of what it reports (Wittgenstein 1963, § 265).
18. Peter Hacker has also emphasized another point that might be of importance to our discussion of Wittgensteinian externalism. In *Insight and Illusion* he thus argues against the "community interpretation" in the following way: "Far from suggesting that a language of a socially isolated individual is inconceivable, because language is always a social activity involving rules that only a social institution can provide, Wittgenstein had no objection to following a rule privately (in solitude), but only to following a 'private' rule, i.e. a rule which no one else *could in principle* understand or follow" (Hacker 1997, pp. 252-253). Undoubtedly it is correct that Wittgenstein had no objection to someone following a rule in solitude. But then it is not clear that any defender of the community view would claim this. Surely, what they would claim is that it makes sense for isolated individuals to follow rules, but only because of the stabilizing framework provided by their membership of (or one-time initiation into) a community. One might also feel that there is something strange about the positive side of Hacker's claim (though it seems corroborated by Wittgenstein 1963, § 256 and elsewhere). He writes: "What is ruled out in the private language argument is not the imaginary soliloquist (solitary or in groups) but one whose concepts, rules, and opinions are essentially unsharable rather than contingently unshared" (Hacker 1997, p. 253). And again: "What is essential is the *possibility* of another's mastering the 'language' that the solitary person 'speaks'" (Baker and

Hacker 1985, p. 175). On this interpretation, what sort of view is Wittgenstein actually arguing against? To be more precise, what would it mean to conceive of a rule that only one person could *in principle* follow? Or of concepts (a "language") that only one speaker could *in principle* understand? If I were the most intelligent person alive, say, I might devise a code (or a rule) so complicated that no other existing person could possibly learn it. But still, it would not be impossible for others *per se* to understand my code (or rule); there might be born a *Wunderkind* tomorrow who would be able to learn it, and so forth. But note the example that Wittgenstein seems to be focused on throughout his discussion of private languages: he is focusing on a language for sensations, or rather, for sensations conceived of in a very special way, as we will see shortly. His reflections, in other words, concern rules and concepts that would be impossible for others to understand, *not* because they were too complicated (or whatever), because here it is hard to see what "in principle" might mean, but rather *because the "objects" these rules and concepts would involve reference to would essentially be accessible only to the private linguist and no one else*. Wittgenstein's idea of a "private language", then, is the idea of a language designed to refer to objects essentially inaccessible to a possible community. This is crucial to the "external" private language argument, which I will discuss shortly.

19. This Wittgensteinian "externalism", whatever its correct formulation, has obvious affinities with Kant's famous "refutation of idealism". Kant, too, was concerned to articulate (what we might call) a kind of externalism. In support of his statement that my consciousness of myself proves the existence of external spatial things, Kant argued: "I am conscious of my own existence as determined in time. All determination of time presupposes something *permanent* in perception. This permanent cannot, however, be something in me, since it is only through this permanent that my existence in time can itself be determined. Thus perception of this permanent is possible only through a *thing* outside me and not through the mere *representation* of a thing outside me; and consequently the determination of my existence in time is possible only through the existence of actual things which I perceive outside me" (Kant 1929, B 275-276). Disregarding the details of Kant's *argument*, one could call the position sketched in this passage, if it were transformed so as to suit our semantic discussion, "Kantian externalism" (cf. Rudd 2003, pp. 49-53). Kantian externalism thus stipulates that there cannot be linguistic meaning unless there is something external to the individual – something more than mere *Vorstellungen* or "representations", something independent of the individual's *Vorstellungen*, something *real*.

20. Indeed, McDowell claims that "the fundamental thrust of Wittgenstein's attack is not to eliminate the idea of a private language", but rather to establish "the general moral: a bare presence cannot be a ground for anything" (McDowell 1996, p. 19). As we will see shortly, the idea of grounding language on "a bare presence" is precisely what the stage-setting considerations push the would-be private linguist toward embracing.

21. There is not much doubt as to how Hegel would respond to this. Indeed, the whole discussion bears striking resemblances to Hegel's discussion of "sense-certainty" in the *Phenomenology of Spirit* – a fact rarely noticed by commentators (but see Putnam 1981, p. 62). The purely "sensory" consciousness, in Hegel's scenario, "has" something, despite its complete lack of general concepts – but what? Well, *this*. But *everything* is a "this" (the pure "this" has no "neighbors", as the middle Wittgenstein would say), so *nothing* in particular has been picked out.

22. See Stern 1995, pp. 175-186 and McGinn 1997, pp. 126-134 for good discussions of these issues.

23. I have corrected the translation here. Luckhardt and Aue translate: "there is no grasping or un-

derstanding of an object, only the grasping of a technique". As if one cannot grasp the object – the colored patch – at all! Wittgenstein, however, writes: "Es gibt hier kein Erfassen, Auffassen des Gegenstandes, außer durch ein Erfassen einer Technik". That is, one *can* of course grasp the object, but *only through* grasping a technique.

24. This is not precisely Malcolm's way of putting it, but I think it preserves the structural distinction he makes. Note that Wittgenstein himself speaks of a "direct" and an "indirect" way of realizing the impossibility of a private ostensive definition (Wittgenstein 1980a, § 397).
25. One philosopher who seems to draw this erroneous conclusion is Richard Rorty (1979, p. 111).
26. McGinn does not endorse this interpretation, but she apparently thinks it is so close to home that it is better to look for an interpretation of Wittgenstein's argument that avoids mentioning "public criteria" for "inner processes" altogether (McGinn 1997, p. 130).
27. I have developed these ideas in greater detail in Overgaard 2005.
28. "Mentalism" is here just realism concerning the mind – that is, the view that *there really are pains, itches, thoughts, perception, emotions*, etc., and that these are non-reducible mental phenomena. If "mentalism" is thought to carry Cartesian metaphysical commitments, then Wittgenstein would be anything but sympathetic to the term (cf. Overgaard 2004).
29. But, if not behaviorism, is this then not at least a questionable "public domain positivism" (cf. Strawson 1994, pp. 308-324)? Perhaps it is, and I am not sure I would want to defend Wittgenstein all the way here. Nevertheless, there is an important core of truth in Wittgenstein's parable, which I will make use of later in this paper.
30. That he is not expounding a general theory of what meaning "is" should be clear. Wittgenstein's choice of words is remarkable. He hardly ever says that meaning *is* or *consists* in use (or anything of the sort); rather, his remarks are of the type: "*one could explain* the meaning of the word 'meaning' by saying…"; "*look upon* the use as…"; "*let* the application teach you…"; etc. His remarks are often more like stage directions in the text of a play than they are propositions expressing philosophical theses!
31. Needless to say, a host of Wittgenstein interpreters would tell us that we may *not* put it in such terms. Often such interpreters base their warnings and restrictions on the fundamental assumption that it is wrong to view Wittgenstein as setting "substantive tasks for philosophy" at all (see, e.g., McDowell 1996, pp. 175-176). I wonder how philosophers such as McDowell can then view themselves as anything remotely like faithful followers of Wittgenstein. Is there no substantive philosophy in *Mind and World*? As far as I can see, the answer can only be negative if it is assumed that "substantive philosophy" (or "traditional philosophy", another favored term for what has to be abandoned) is identical with a very limited set of problems (several of them inherited from Descartes). But just a little familiarity with philosophical traditions outside of the mainstream of analytic philosophy should convince one that this assumption is questionable.
32. Not only that; Rudd's brief, but illuminating discussion of McCulloch's interpretation of Wittgenstein (Rudd 1997, and 2003, pp. 80-84) is an important source of inspiration for this paper.
33. Incidentally, McCulloch's critical remarks on this aspect of Putnam's argument suggest that one should not assume out of hand that McCulloch's externalism is simply identical with "Putnamian externalism". Rudd, however, seems to me to do just that. That is probably also why he feels he can declare that Putnam has later "abandoned 'Putnamian externalism' altogether" (Rudd 1997, p. 502), when in fact Putnam reiterates the central points of his semantic externalism as late as in 1999 (Putnam 1999, pp. 119-120). What Putnam (of the 1999 vintage, and indeed already the 1981 vintage; cf. Putnam 1981, chapter 3) *has* abandoned is just the realism that McCulloch wants to emphasize to such an extent that he cannot but be dissatisfied even with Putnam's original presentation of the issues in "The Meaning of 'Meaning'".

34. The two responses to Rudd that I have sketched here rest on misunderstandings of his argument, but misunderstandings that Rudd does not do enough to rule out.
35. Of course, McCulloch does not claim that human language, and the human form of life as such, is concerned with *nothing but* the tracking of the hidden reality of things (cf. McCulloch 1995, p. 210). But the more modest claim that *part* of what our form of life "does" is to track essences also seems to imply a dubious intellectualization of human life.
36. McCulloch would know how to reply to such a critique. As he writes, "people who become irritated at such procedures [i.e., 'imaginary counter-examples'] simply have no proper grasp of what enquiry is all about. Nor is this just a point about *philosophical* enquiry: thought-experiment is an integral part of scientific theorising too. Only politicians and other simpletons who need the comfort of easy answers refuse to consider hypothetical questions" (McCulloch 1995, p. 174).
37. See Putnam 1999, p. 54. It is interesting that Putnam himself, following the lead of Wittgenstein and Austin (among others), has recently adopted this view, abandoning metaphysical realism but (unlike in Putnam 1981) upholding what he calls "natural realism".
38. In his critique of metaphysical realism in *Reason, Truth and History*, Putnam emphasizes that realism presupposes what he calls "a God's Eye point of view" (Putnam 1981, pp. 49-50). In this book it is the metaphysical realistic outlook that Putnam labels "externalism" (precisely because it holds that it is possible to achieve an external point of view on mind, language, and world), while his own perspective is labeled "internalism" (holding that no such external viewpoint is possible). On such a classificatory scheme, of course, the Wittgenstein I have presented does come out as an "internalist". A good discussion of these two very different internalism-externalism oppositions – together with the interesting suggestion that Searle's argument in favor of a full-blooded internalism trades on confusing the two oppositions – is found in McDowell 1998, pp. 270-274.
39. This study was funded by the Carlsberg Foundation and carried out at the Danish National Research Foundation: *Center for Subjectivity Research*, University of Copenhagen. I have benefited from comments made by Dan Zahavi, Thor Grünbaum, and Lisa Käll. Needless to say, however, I alone am responsible for the (numerous) problems and obscurities that continue to beset this paper.

References

Austin, J. L. (1979) *Philosophical Papers*. Ed. J. O. Urmson and G. J. Warnock. Oxford: Oxford University Press.
Baker, G. P. and Hacker, P. M. S. (1984) *Skepticism, Rules and Language*. Oxford: Blackwell.
Baker, G. P. and Hacker, P. M. S. (1985) *Wittgenstein: Rules, Grammar, and Necessity*. Oxford: Blacwell.
Budd, M. (1989) *Wittgenstein's Philosophy of Psychology*. London: Routledge.
Burge, T. (1979) "Individualism and the Mental". *Midwest Studies in Philosophy* 4: 73-121.
Crary, A. (2000) "Introduction". In A. Crary and R. Read (eds.), *The New Wittgenstein*, pp. 1-18. London: Routledge.
Fogelin, R. J. (1976) *Wittgenstein*. London: Routledge.
Hacker, P. M. S. (1997) *Insight and Illusion: Themes in the Philosophy of Wittgenstein*. Bristol: Thoemmes Press.
Kant, I. (1929) *Critique of Pure Reason*. Trans. Norman Kemp Smith. London: Macmillan.
Kenny, A. (1975) *Wittgenstein*. Harmondsworth, Middlesex: Penguin.
Kripke, S. (1982) *Wittgenstein on Rules and Private Language*. Oxford: Blackwell.

Malcolm, N. (1966) "Wittgenstein's *Philosophical Investigations*" In Pitcher (ed.), *Wittgenstein: The Philosophical Investigations*, pp. 65-103. Garden City NY: Anchor Books.
McCulloch, G. (1995) *The Mind and Its World*. London: Routledge.
McCulloch, G. (2003) *The Life of the Mind: An Essay on Phenomenological Externalism*. London: Routledge.
McDowell, J. (1996) *Mind and World*. 2nd, expanded edition. Cambridge, Mass.: Harvard University Press.
McDowell, J. (1998) *Meaning, Knowledge, and Reality*. Cambridge, Mass.: Harvard University Press.
McGinn, C. (1984) *Wittgenstein on Meaning: An Interpretation and Evaluation*. Oxford: Basil Blackwell.
McGinn, M. (1997) *Wittgenstein and the Philosophical Investigations*. London: Routledge.
Overgaard, S. (2004) "Exposing the Conjuring Trick: Wittgenstein on Subjectivity", *Phenomenology and the Cognitive Sciences* 3: 263-286.
Overgaard, S. (2005) "Rethinking Other Minds: Wittgenstein and Levinas on Expression", forthcoming in *Inquiry*.
Pears, D. (1988) *The False Prison: A Study of the Development of Wittgenstein's Philosophy. Volume II*. Oxford: Clarendon Press.
Putnam, H. (1975) *Mind, Language, and Reality: Philosophical Papers, Vol. 2*. Cambridge: Cambridge University Press.
Putnam, H. (1981) *Reason, Truth and History*. Cambridge: Cambridge University Press.
Putnam, H. (1988) *Representation and Reality*. Cambridge, Mass.: MIT Press.
Putnam, H. (1999) *The Threefold Cord: Mind, Body, and World*. New York: Columbia University Press.
Rorty, R. (1979) *Philosophy and the Mirror of Nature*. Princeton: Princeton University Press.
Rudd, A. (1997) "Two Types of Externalism". *Philosophical Quarterly* 47: 501-507.
Rudd, A. (2003) *Expressing the World: Skepticism, Wittgenstein, and Heidegger*. Chicago: Open Court.
Savigny, E. von. (1996) *Der Mensch als Mitmensch: Wittgensteins "Philosophische Untersuchungen"*. Munich: Deutscher Taschenbuch Verlag.
Searle, J. (1983) *Intentionality: An Essay in the Philosophy of Mind*. Cambridge: Cambridge University Press.
Stern, D. G. (1995) *Wittgenstein on Mind and Language*. New York: Oxford University Press.
Strawson, G. (1994) *Mental Reality*. Cambridge, Mass.: The MIT Press.
Williams, M. (1999) *Wittgenstein, Mind, and Meaning: Towards a Social Conception of Mind*. London: Routledge.
Wittgenstein, L. (1958) *The Blue and Brown Books*. Ed. R. Rhees. Oxford: Blackwell.
Wittgenstein, L. (1963) *Philosophical Investigations*. Trans. G. E. M. Anscombe. Oxford: Blackwell.
Wittgenstein, L. (1978) *Remarks on the Foundations of Mathematics*. Ed. G. H. von Wright, R. Rhees, and G. E. M. Anscombe, trans. G. E. M. Anscombe. Oxford: Blackwell.
Wittgenstein, L. (1980a) *Remarks on the Philosophy of Psychology*, Volume I. Ed. G. E. M. Anscombe and G. H. von Wright, trans. G. E. M. Anscombe. Oxford: Blackwell.
Wittgenstein, L. (1980b) *Remarks on the Philosophy of Psychology*, Volume II. Ed. G. H. von Wright and H. Nyman, trans. C. G. Luckhardt and M. A. E. Aue. Oxford: Blackwell.
Wittgenstein, L. (1982) *Last Writings on the Philosophy of Psychology*, Volume I. Ed. G. H. von Wright and H. Nyman, trans. C. G. Luckhardt and M. A. E. Aue. Oxford: Blackwell.
Wittgenstein, L. (1992) *Last Writings on the Philosophy of Psychology*; Volume II. Ed G. H. von Wright and H. Nyman, trans. C. G. Luckhardt and M. A. E. Aue. Oxford: Blackwell.

OUT OF HARM'S WAY?

MORTEN EBBE JUUL NIELSEN

Section for Philosophy and Science Studies
Roskilde University Centre

I: Introductory Remarks and Abstract

This article deals with the alleged connection between two well known topics in political philosophy, the harm principle and liberal neutrality. The claim under consideration is that the harm principle – or more precisely, the concept of harm – can function as a neutral watershed between legitimate and illegitimate modes of reasoning and arguments, insofar that the concept of harm can illuminate and buttress the distinction between the right and the good necessary for neutralism. I offer a negative appraisal of this claim.

Allegiance to the harm principle – in Mill's words: "…the only purpose for which power can be rightfully exercised over any member of a civilised community…is to prevent harm to others" – seems to be a watershed between liberals and their opponents. Rather surprisingly, only few contemporary mainstream liberals have provided in-depth discussion or defence of the principle. Nevertheless, it is often invoked by liberals, at least in everyday political debates. "Why should we not outlaw homosexual or other unusual sexual practices between consenting adults, or forbid publication of *Why I am not a Muslim*"? "Because no one is harmed", is the default liberal answer. In short, the harm principle, in one version or another expresses a fundamental liberal concern for liberty and anti-paternalism (cf.: Holtug, p. 357.)

As well as some sort of allegiance to the harm principle, many contemporary liberals hold a version of the principle of *neutrality of justification*. In short, this is the idea that state actions are only legitimate if they are backed up solely by (adequate) reasons and arguments that do not rely on a, or some, specific ideal(s) about the good (life.)

Now, It might be suggested – indeed, it seems to be the case that it has[1] – that the harm principle can function as an adequately neutral moral principle that helps us to distinguish between valid (i.e., neutral) and invalid (i.e., non-neutral) reasons for state actions. In a nutshell, the contention is that if some action plausibly falls under the concept of harming (someone else), then state coercion (or law making in general) vis-à-vis that action is *neutrally justifi-*

able, at least *ceteris paribus*. This presupposes that there is a neutral conceptualisation of harm, i.e., that there is a credible idea of harm that is innocent vis-à-vis different ideas of the good (life); otherwise, a specific (liberal) conception of the good would be smuggled in to the very core of neutralism.

In this article, I challenge this idea. I contend that any plausible concept of harm or harming involves specific and possibly controversial ideas of the good; or, that it relies on the specific theory of justice which it is supposed to support, and hence, that appeals to the independent justificatory power of the concept of harm remains circular. Hence, neutralists cannot use the harm principle as a neutral dividing line between valid and invalid reasons for state action. Furthermore, I believe that even liberals who do not adhere to the principle of justificatory neutrality, but nevertheless believe that the harm principle is an uncontroversial principle will have to give up that idea in the light of the arguments given here.

II: The Doctrine of Justificatory Neutrality and the Right – Good Distinction

First, we must define the doctrine of neutrality: I shall take "neutrality" in this context to mean neutrality of justification (hereafter: N), the idea that conceptions of the good cannot legitimately form part of state justifications of state actions (…laws, institutions, etc.) In a phrase, N – the absence of conceptions of the good in chains of arguments (purportedly) justifying state actions – is a necessary condition for state *legitimacy*.

I bypass here some otherwise pertinent issues concerning the scope and precise interpretation of N (I believe that the arguments in the following are relevant for all plausible interpretations of N):

- Does N apply to the entire range of laws and institutions (what might be dubbed *principled neutrality*) or only to "questions of constitutional essentials and basic matters of justice" (Rawls (1993), p.214, see also Rawls (2001), pp. 90f) (what might be called *limited neutrality*.) In the latter case: how and why do we distinguish between the "spheres of neutrality" and the rest; especially, how do we do so in a neutral manner?
- Should the defence of N be neutral itself (this we might call *theoretical neutrality*), or could the defence be partly or wholly buttressed by a, or some, conceptions of the good (We might call this *political neutrality*)[2] without fatally compromising N?
- There are several routes – moral or pragmatic arguments – that could lead

different theorists to N,[3] and the way N is understood will inevitably reflect the route leading to it.

In the context of this article, I will take the strongest version (i.e., principled, theoretical neutrality) to be the default position of N[4], and I shall remain silent regarding the broader justification of N as such.

The main idea of N, then, is that conceptions of the good cannot adequately form part of a justification for state actions. Only conceptions of the *right,* or justice, can justify state actions.

Hence, N builds on (or necessitates) the idea that our normative playing field can be neatly divided into two separate parts, the spheres of justice and the good:

> [The distinction between the right and the good] is integral to neutralist liberalism, for in so far it advocates official government neutrality between competing conceptions of the good, it implicitly assumes that we can delineate the area of the right, and then move on to resolving questions about the good life and the forms it may take.[5]

In order for neutralism to be a successful enterprise, it is imperative that this division can be spelled out in and on terms that are 1) at least reasonably clear-cut; otherwise, the doctrine fails to provide us with understandable and workable criteria for distinguishing between valid and invalid reasons (arguments, values, conceptions…) for state actions, and 2) at least reasonably *neutral* (between different conceptions of the good); otherwise, the division will reflect ideas about political validity held true by adherents of only some conceptions of the good, hence compromising neutrality from the outset.

Now, it might be asked why this should pose a great challenge in the first place. Is not the distinction between the right and the good adequately clear and neutral between conceptions of the good? Many believe that this is not so.[6]

One of the sources of worry about the cogency of the right – good distinction is that it is inherently and inescapably fuzzy, because any conceptualisation of either of the spheres will reflect ideas belonging to the other: my ideas about justice are shaped by my ideas about the good, and vice versa.[7]

Another is the question why we should accept or believe that the line of demarcation between valid (i.e., reasons of the right or justice) and invalid (i.e., of the good) reasons tracks both the division between uncontroversial and controversial reasons and the division between universalisable (objective or public) and subjective (private) reasons.[8] It is not at all clear that conceptions of justice are any less controversial, or less disputable, than conceptions of the good (cf.: Hurka, p. 163.) Furthermore, it is not at all clear that conceptions of justice are less epistemologically unreliable (or "transparent", in Bird's phrase)[9] than conceptions of the good: Neutralists' scepticism concerning the universalisability of *all* conceptions of the good seems to be more of a case of *fiat* than actual rational argument. In short: neutralists have failed to provide a defence of the idea that conceptions of justice are more epistemically trustworthy and less controversial than conceptions of the good.

A third worry can be described as follows: insofar as neutrality is a "gag-rule" (Holmes, p.24), forbidding discussion or at least justification proceeding from ideas of the good, it seems that neutrality is dogmatically putting off the agenda competing political theories, e.g., perfectionist, republican, communitarian or socialists perspectives. In itself, this is not a problem, for any political theory must hold itself to be the superior one, even a theory as irenic in spirit as liberal neutrality. However, this poses a special challenge for liberal neutralism: seen from "the outside", i.e., from a competing political theory, it will always seem to be the case that *their* specific ideas of the good are left off the agenda simply by neutralist *fiat*, and that this exclusion is itself motivated (and only defensible) in terms of a special, liberal neutralist conceptions of the good. Neutralists fail to deal with the objection that the *political* scheme following from neutrality is far from impartial between those citizens who endorse such a scheme and those who do not. Clearly, neutrality does not aim to be neutral (in the generic sense) between different conceptions of the political, or "third-person-ethics". However, some citizens' views of the political are grounded inseparably in their views of "first-person-ethics" or conceptions of the good; hence, neutrality is not neutral among conceptions of the good: it caters only to citizens who endorse the conceptions of the good supportive of or compatible with the political arrangements of neutrality.[10]

I will not directly try to deal with these objections to the cogency of the right – good distinction and N here. The point of the exercise is to make it clear that neutralists *do* need to provide their critics with some kind of defence of the distinction between the right and the good.[11]

Where do the harm principle and the concept of harm fit into this gamut of problems? They do so as an attempt to make the distinction between valid and invalid reasons – i.e., the right – good distinction – clearer and more neutral, and as an attempt to find an independent line of justification buttressing the doctrine of neutrality as such. It seems uncontroversial to claim that, since "harming" is *prima* facie wrong, then the state is *ceteris paribus* (by no means necessarily) justified in taking action to prevent harm. If the concept of harm is neutral between competing, acceptable conceptions of the good, it seems that we can justify state actions to prevent harm in a neutrally satisfying manner and philosophically, we make it clear(-er) which kinds of reasons and arguments are acceptable for the neutralist. To see whether the harm principle or the concept of harm can play such a role, we need to examine those concepts more closely.

III: Harm and the Harm Principle

The concept of harm and the harm principle are clearly controversial matters. There is a host of questions pertinent to any clarification of them; important among these are:
- What kinds of coercion does the principle rule out?
- Should we understand the principle in such terms that coercion is justified *ex post*; only if harm was *actually* prevented (or reduced) was coercion justified, or should we rather understand it *ex ante*: coercion is justified if it (typically) prevents or reduces *risk* of harm?
- Should we understand the principle as *origin-centred*: the person harming (or potentially harming) is the only proper object of coercion, or should we understand it as *origin-neutral*: that it justifies coercion of persons who are not the cause of harm in order to prevent or reduce (risk of) harm?
- Should we understand the principle as justifying only coercion of people who *do* harm, or should we take it to encompass justified coercion of people who *allow* harm as well?
- Should we accept the standard liberal assumption that the harm principle justifies coercion only when *other* agents are harmed by the harming agent, or should we broaden the scope to include justification of coercion to prevent or reduce (risk of) harm to one self? (For these and related problems of clarification of the harm principle, see Holtug, pp. 360ff.)

However, I shall concentrate on another, fundamental problem, namely, the definition of (relevant) harm as such.

However, some initial comments are in order. I shall take the idea, or perhaps the spirit, of the harm principle, to be the following: the state ought not to interfere coercively in the life of a given citizen in order to promote a specific kind of moral code or conduct, other than the specific kind of moral code necessary for the prevention of (risk of) harm to others. This is (*ceteris paribus*, at least) the *only* justification of state coercion.[12]

Furthermore, the relevant concept of "harm" must involve something more than outcry, indignation, irritation, or annoyance. "Mere knowledge" of something – e.g. that my neighbour gulps down coke with oysters – cannot count as harm. A's *belief* that it is bad that someone else, B, does, or does not, undertake some action Φ,[13] cannot in itself count as harm. In essence, the harm principle tries to capture the traditional liberal concern for individual liberty vis-à-vis the state: the state should only interfere when someone's interests are *truly* threatened or diminished; when someone's *own* life is made worse off by someone else's actions. Hence, according to any reasonable liberal interpretation of the harm principle, I cannot complain that *I* am harmed in any relevant sense by other people's behaviour, sexual mores, codes of conduct, manners, beliefs (religious and otherwise), unless this affects me in a way which causally sets back my interests.[14]

The concept of harm relevant to the harm principle, then, cannot take any and all preferences of citizens to be *reasons* for state actions. Perhaps I have a preference – even a very strong, dominant preference – that no one quaffs fizzy drinks with seafood. Knowing that my neighbour does so might even harm me (in some sort of generic sense) insofar I get terribly upset to the degree where my other important projects are frustrated. But this cannot count as *relevant* harm: counting such preferences would inevitably restrict the individual liberty which the principle sets out to protect in a much too strong way.

A way of trying to catch this difference in a satisfying manner is to distinguish between *self-* and *other-regarding* preferences or desires (see Dworkin (1977), p. 234; (1985b); Kymlicka (1990), pp. 36f.) The gist of the suggestion is familiar: We should not count preferences regarding the lives and conducts of *others* – they are simply put off the agenda in constructing and evaluating political institutions and theories – rather, we should concentrate exclusively on *self-regarding* desires or preferences. Hence, (relevant) harm is only harm to (frustration of) self-regarding preferences. However, this will not do: It might be the case that my desire that my neighbour does not have coke with his seafood is essentially other-regarding; but *I* have the second-order desire about *my* desires that they should not be frustrated, and hence, even my *self*-regarding desires are frustrated by my neighbours culinary incompetence (Holtug, p.365.) Furthermore, this whole line of reasoning builds upon the premise that preferences are the prime building block (or at least a prominent one) for our normative theory, and many, including myself, would disagree that this is the case. Thus, the distinction between self- and other regarding desires or preferences does not provide a short-cut to a satisfactory conception of relevant harm.

In short, there seems to be no obvious way of defining harm in a way which does not involve a more *substantial* discussion of the concept. Furthermore, a conceptualisation of harm or the harm principle which does not sufficiently capture the liberal spirit mentioned in the above cannot be right for neutralist purposes, insofar as neutralism is a *liberal* aspiration.[15]

IV: Harm and Neutrality

As pointed out in (II), neutralists need to provide a good explanation of the alleged schism between conceptions of the right and conceptions of the good. I have mentioned that this explanation must be clear-cut (otherwise, we lack a workable criterion for distinguishing between valid and invalid reasons) and neutral (otherwise, neutrality is compromised from the beginning). But some more comments are due.

The fundamental challenge to any plausible conceptualisation of N is to find a way to formulate and defend the theory which is truly (or adequately)[16] neutral between competing acceptable[17] conceptions of the good. An essential component of that enterprise must be to formulate the distinction between valid and invalid reasons (i.e., the right – good distinction) for state actions in a way conforming to the demands just enumerated. Note also that this should be done in a way which is suitably *independent* of other parts of the neutralist theory; notably, it must be independent of the theory of justice given by most neutralists: it is not an adequate explanation of the distinction that it is necessitated by the distributive theory which it is supposed to make clear. Somehow, the distinction must be explained and justified in terms that are sufficiently independent of the theory which is erected upon it.

To illustrate: often, neutralist theorists invoke the concept of "reasonable" in order to explain the difference between valid and invalid reasons and arguments. Only reasonable arguments and moral conceptions should form the basis of a liberal political morality, and neutrality is only meant to apply to reasonable conceptions of the good (e.g., the theory is not meant to be neutral between conceptions of the good that emphasise peaceful coexistence and cooperation and conceptions that are not.) (See. e.g., Rawls (1993), pp. 49f, 61f, but compare: Dworkin (1995), p. 215 *et circa.*)

However, one looks in vain for successful arguments to the effect that the concept of reasonable is in itself adequately neutral between conceptions of the good and/or that it could be conceived in a neutral manner. This means that one must look deeper for a justification of the distinction between valid and invalid, the right and the good.

It is here the suggestion that the concept of harm and the harm principle can play a role as a *neutral* way of distinguishing between valid and invalid reasons, and to make the distinction between the right and the good clearer. *Prima facie,* this sounds like a plausible suggestion: after all, should not all (reasonable – there we go again…) conceptions of the good come to the same conclusions about what is truly harmful? Is not the concept of harm less controversial, less epistemically uncertain, and more apt to generate consensus than, e.g., ideals about character or ignobleness etc.?

In the following, I shall claim that this is not the case. I argue that the neutralist move – to search for an independent concept of harm that is adequately neutral between competing conceptions of the good, which can be used to explain and justify the right – good distinction – founders for one of two reasons: either, the concept of harm *is* independent of the rest of the neutralist framework, notably the theory of justice normally accompanying the idea of liberal neutrality. But in that case, the concept is bound to be intimately linked to a, or some, conceptions of the good, hence undermining the claim to neutrality. Alternatively, the concept of harm is tailored in some way in which it is plausible to call it neutral between competing conceptions of the good. However, the price paid for this is complete lack of independence from the theory which it was supposed to explain and justify. Hence, the concept of harm is either irrelevant or superfluous and circular.

V: The Definition of Harm: Good-oriented or Circular

So, the question at this juncture is: can we have a neutral and freestanding (i.e., non-circular) concept of harm? The kind of neutrality involved is of course not complete moral neutrality – that is impossible – but it must not rely on conceptions of the good. Almost needless to say, it must also be an attractive conception; e.g., it must fit with our intuitions or accepted facts about harm as well as with other well-considered theoretical and moral propositions.

As an analytical tool, we might differentiate between *moralised* and *non-moralised* concepts of harm.[18] In turn:

A Non-moralised Conception of Harm

In formulating a non-moralised conception of harm, one would try to avoid mentioning concepts like right or wrong, (morally) good and bad, wrongdoing, and the like, and try to concentrate on giving a purely *prudential* definition of harm: what would be harmful as such to human beings.[19] Clearly, this is a discussion related to theories of well-being, or welfare. However, adopting a specific theory of well-being is dangerous for the neutralist: in one standard formulation, the principle of neutrality must be blind to the specific *philosophical* doctrines held by citizens (Rawls (1971), p.212; Rawls (1993), p.223.) This formula seems *prima facie* puzzling; for, of course, the moral doctrine of neutrality is itself a philosophical doctrine. The quandary is somewhat alleviated when it is remembered that Rawls (at least from *Political Liberalism* and onwards) does not believe that *truth* is the right criterion for the adequacy of Justice as Fairness; rather, the theory must be *reasonable* (for this, see Mulhall/Swift, pp. 233ff; Raz (1994).) In the light of this, it is tempting to say that, in Rawls' idiom, "philosophical" theories are theories involving truth as a standard of correctness, whereas Justice as Fairness (and neutralist theory in general?) involves reasonableness as the standard of correctness.

Even granting the soundness of this theoretical construct (something I am not inclined to do, but let us proceed anyway), this entangles the neutralist in an unpleasant web. On one hand, we want our theory of well-being to be *true* for individuals; if we are talking about personal well-being (remember that we examining a non-moralised or prudential concept of harm), we would want the derivative concept of harm to ring true, in some sense, in the ears of individuals. We are not talking about – not straightforwardly, anyway – what individuals *ought* to count as reductions of well-being (harm), but *what actually is* reduction of well-being.[20] But such comprehensive conceptions of *the good* are pre-eminently controversial and hardly fitting elements in an overlapping consensus of the kind envisaged by Rawls *et al.* On the other hand, trying to incorporate elements of (e.g.) what we as citizens *ought* to accept given we want to find an overlapping consensus (Rawls), or that we ought to opt for conditions of optimal equality (Dworkin, Ackerman), or to that we ought to accept in order to respect each other's equal status as independent, rational beings

(Dworkin, Larmore), into the theory of the good needed as a foil for the concept of harm changes the concept of harm into a moralised one (where it will encounter different insurmountable problems.)

There are other lines of thought apart from the one just sketched that should persuade the critic that neutralists cannot rely on a non-moralised concept of harm.

Consider, for instance, the inevitable differences in ideas about the proper way to circumscribe political power that will arise from different persons' ideas about the good, and the accompanying ideas about what should count as harm. In general, the neutralist model of the proper circumscription of political power tracks the (distinctively liberal) distinction between public and private matters (Nielsen (2003); Edmundson, part III); which is modelled over the distinction between the right – good distinction (or vice versa.) What belongs to the private sphere cannot form part of the justificatory background for a neutralist liberal order; only "public" conceptions can do so. Politics – political matters – accordingly stops at the doorstep of the "private sphere." However, non-neutralist liberals and non-liberals as such will most often disagree with the neutralist liberal about this: perfectionist liberals (and many feminists, republicans, and socialists) will complain that the distinction between public and personal morality is bogus, or at least itself a proper subject for political discussion. The conceptions of the good of many non-neutralists (republicans and communitarians, for instance) include the idea that political participation and the possibility of expressing matters normally associated with personal morality on a political and legal level are important values, and that they in a relevant sense are *harmed* by the neutralists' alleged exclusion of personal morality from the political agenda.[21] In short, neutralists (still) owe critics a good answer to the following challenge: in what sense is liberal neutrality neutral vis-à-vis citizens whose conception of the *political good* (and the corresponding picture of harm) differs from the one expressed by the neutralist political regime?

Even without the burden of having to manoeuvre with the demand of neutrality, the quest for a plausible non-moralised concept of harm encounters severe problems.

We cannot define harm for neutralist purposes exclusively in terms of reduction of (positive) welfare (or prevention of increases of negative welfare) (see Holtug, pp. 364f.) If we take the three dominant theories to be hedonism, preference-satisfaction, and perfectionism, respectively, we encounter the following challenges: Hedonism cannot serve as the basis for the harm principle if we want the principle to prevent the state from interfering in practices of consensual sexual action. An agent offended by certain sexual practices will, on this prudential conception of harm, be harmed by knowledge of other agents performing these practices. But this kind of harm is exactly what the harm principle – and hence: the concept of harm that we are looking for – cannot include. Preference-satisfaction theories fare no better, as we saw in the discussion of self- and other-regarding desires or preferences. Moving into the field of perfectionist or objective list-theories of wellbeing, it seems to be the case that any plausible such theory must include, among other things, pleasurable mental states. Hence, it will involve itself in the same problems as the other theories.[22]

Furthermore, it is at least an open question whether any of these theories of wellbeing are thoroughly independent of conceptions of the good in their formulation.[23] E.g., is it really plausible that the building blocks of hedonism, pain and pleasure and their intensity is conceivable independently of some pretty substantial descriptions of the good? Maybe there is a physiological basis for pain that is adequately neutral between all plausible conceptions of the good, but the phenomenological appearance of pain seems to me to be importantly bound to conceptions of the good. Any sufficiently precise rendering of "pain" and its intensity is intimately linked with both cultural and personal conceptions of frustration of goals, which again are bound up with conceptions of the good. For instance, my slight backache might be physiologically identical to the sensations of a devoted basketball player, but whereas I experience only a minor nuisance, the backache of the basketball player might prevent him from exercising his most important goals.

Leaving aside the pertinent problems regarding adopting a theory of wellbeing or welfare that suits neutralist purposes, it is conceivable that the neutralist would argue that it is not any old reduction of welfare which is relevant for our concept of harm and the harm principle; rather, it is a certain *amount* of harm that is relevant (see Holtug, pp.365ff.) After all, it might be argued that the *amount* of harm involved in certain acts fall below a certain threshold; a "threshold of relevance", so to speak. So, only harm which exceeds the threshold would count as relevant harm. The gist of such a suggestion would be that the amount of harm involved in, e.g., knowing that my neighbour drinks fizzy drinks with his seafood falls below the threshold, whereas the harm involved in, say, you hitting me in the head is (normally) above. However, the drawing of the line seems pretty random: if, say, we draw the line at 50 units of pain, so that a reduction of welfare of 49 units is acceptable, whereas a reduction of 50 justifies coercion, it is always relevant to ask the question "how can a mere difference of one unit make a difference in *kind* such that warranted coercion suddenly emerges?" (Holtug, p. 366; Kagan, pp.81f.)

To sum up: non-moralised or prudential conceptions of harm do not do the trick for the neutralist. The main problem is that any conception of harm spelled out in terms of wellbeing will inevitably end up relying on some specific ideas about the good, hence compromising neutrality. Non-moralised concepts of harm are essentially good-oriented.

The arguments put forward in the above, and further related problems about the proper baseline for judging something to be a loss of welfare (see Holtug, pp. 366ff) point in the (perhaps unsurprising) direction that we must move from a purely prudential conception of harm to a *moralised* conception. In a phrase, this means moving from a concept of mere harm to a concept of *wrongdoing*. For, on the standard liberal and neutralist model, the reason that no one is harmed in the relevant sense in the examples above about consensual sexual practices, the publication of books that might offend religious zealots, and my pesky neighbour, is perhaps not so much that no one is *harmed*; rather, it is that no one is *wronged*. The basic contention is that I do not have a *right* that my neighbour does not have coke with his fish.

A Moralised Conception of Harm

A moralised conception of harm, then, will try to incorporate standards of *justice* into the texture of the needed notion of harm. Basically, moralised conceptions of harm (at least in this context) can take on two different forms: consequentialist and deontological.

Consequentialist attempts to find a neutral conception of harm will fail to yield the wanted results, because there are cases in which the consequentialist framework will demand that the harm principle should be set aside, because more good can be achieved that way. Hence, this version of the harm principle or a concept of harm cannot be used to distinguish between the right and the good in a way that satisfies standard neutralist assumptions about the permissibility of state intervention. Sometimes, the principle will allow interference in the alleged private sphere in order to prevent harmful consequences; hence, it will fail to produce a clear-cut demarcation between the spheres of valid and invalid action and valid and invalid modes of argument.[24]

It will take a little more work to show that the deontological attempts fail in the end:

To reiterate: we are looking for a neutrally satisfactory (i.e., a neutral, clear-cut, and otherwise philosophically and logically sound) conception of the alleged schism between the right and the good. To that end, we turn to the harm principle and the concept of harm. If we can find a conceptualisation of harm that is independent of the neutrality principle, the theory of justice associated with neutralism and which is, in itself, neutral among conceptions of the good, we can use the concept of harm as a neutral watershed between the right and the good.

My claim is that invoking a deontological theory of relevant harm for this purpose will ultimately involve the neutralist in a circular movement. Let us take a look at the harm principle again. It says that (state) coercion is only justified to prevent harm (wrongdoing.) We are now looking for a moralised concept of harm distinguishing, among other things, between mere offence and true harm. For the neutralist, the relevant kind of harm must be violations of agents' *rights*, e.g., a right to privacy, or a right against state paternalism (subject, of course, to the standard riders.) Now, what we are looking for is a conceptualisation of rights that can be said to be in the proper way independent of the right – good distinction (because we are looking for a neutral and independent justification of that distinction itself.) However, it seems that the chain of justification goes in exactly the *opposite* direction: that the rights are justified partly with the help of the right – good distinction. You have a right to Φ or X because the theory of justice says so. Hence, rights cannot be used to justify a certain conception of the right – good distinction insofar we are looking for an independent justification of that distinction.

But could one not say that rights are, in themselves, derivable independently from the right – good distinction? For instance, from the more or less full-blown theory of justice from within they are conceived? Unfortunately for the neutralist, this only involves him in another damaging circularity: At the end of the day, we are looking for a justification of a neutralist theory of justice. This includes, obviously, the principle of neutrality. The challenge to the principle of neutrality is that it relies on a controversial and non-neutral conception of the right – good distinction. In order to find a neutral justification of that, we are looking for a neutral and independent conceptualisation of the concept of harm. This forces the move to a moralised conceptualisation of harm or wrongdoing, which makes us move to the concept of rights. Now, if the concept of *rights* is to be justified by the overarching theory of justice, we are in effect back to square one.

If what we are looking for is a neutral and *freestanding* concept (of harm) to buttress and render clearer the distinction between the right and the good and hence, to support the doctrine of neutrality *which is a part of a conception of justice*, it seems to be the case that we are involved in a blatantly circular enterprise if we incorporate elements of justice in the definition of harm.[25]

Hence, moralised conceptions of harm – this seems to be evident – are not independent of theories of justice or rights or just entitlements. Hence, such concepts of harm hardly give any independent support to the theory of justice which they are *derived* from. In short, attempts to buttress the doctrine of neutrality by appealing to moralised concepts of harm seem inevitably circular: Since "causing harm" entails (morally speaking) that the action is at least "…prima facie wrong, it is a normative concept acquiring its specific meaning from the moral theory within which it is embedded" (Raz (1986), p.414), one cannot use the principle alone to justify a specific normative theory that either rejects or confirms that certain legal measures are morally permissible.

IV: Conclusion

The harm principle, or the concept of harm, is not innocent between different conceptions of the good. Hence, it fits poorly with neutralist theory, because the latter will try to remain uncommitted vis-à-vis competing conceptions of the good. Disconnecting the concept of harm from considerations of the good – in itself an implausible theoretical move, I think – must mean connecting it to an encompassing theory of justice. But then it seems that it is the theory of justice that must do the work by itself, and the concept of harm becomes superfluous. At least, the concept of harm cannot be used to *independently* buttress that theory of justice from which it is derived. Hence, neutralists cannot appeal to the concept of harm as an independent justification of their given specific conception of justice.

I believe these considerations are relevant not only in the ongoing debate about neutralist liberalism, but for other versions of liberalism (and non-liberal theories invoking the harm principle) as well. The harm principle has a certain appealing ring to it; nevertheless, everything interesting about it boils down to the definition of harm. In the end, this is a discussion about goodness and the role that conceptions of goodness ought to or must play in a plausible political theory. Appeals to the harm principle only scratch the surface of a much more complicated and controversial debate.

Notes

1. Pauer-Studer, p.185. Other theorists pointing in that direction (or at least point in the direction that there is a connection between the two ideas) are Neal (1997), p.138; Hart, p.5: Charlesworth, p.45. Cf.: Holtug, pp.362; 362n13. Note that I am not claiming that there is a necessary connection between allegiance to the harm principle and the idea of neutrality of justification.
2. This might sound like a strange phrase. The idea is to emphasise that even neutralists who find it acceptable to defend N in terms of a, or some conceptions of the good would still insist that the *political practice* of N should be (wholly or partly) neutral; hence "political" neutrality.
3. Sher argues persuasively that there are three main classes of arguments leading towards N: Epistemological arguments stressing the alleged rational inconclusiveness of conceptions of the good or their failure to be adequately rationally defensible per se; instrumental or "prophylactic" arguments to the effect that N is the best safeguard against a number of malaises connected with state tyranny and political incompetence; and finally, the most important class, autonomy-based arguments claiming either that a) non-neutrality will have overall detrimental consequences for individual liberty or b) non-neutrality fails to respect individual autonomy as such (Sher, chapters 3-6)
4. Someone might argue that I thereby beg the question against N, especially in the light of Dworkin's (only) political defence of N and Rawls' concessions to limited (and perhaps even only political) N (see Dworkin (1995), *passim*; Rawls (1993), pp. 138, 144, 152ff, 200, 215; (2001), pp.151f.) However, I maintain that the arguments and problems sketched in this article are relevant for even a "watered down" version of N, insofar and to the extent it involves the concept of harm in the way discussed below.
5. Mendus, p.119
6. See Wall, p.100; Raz (1986), pp. 136f; 160f; Neal (1997), pp.34ff.
7. Even though Dworkin is plausibly labelled a neutralist, he points in directions of this critique. See, e.g., Dworkin (1995), p. 214
8. See, e.g., Sher, pp. 37ff, 140ff for these and related discussions
9. Bird (1996) p. 71 *et passim*
10. Someone might retort to these last objections that neutrality is not meant to be neutrality between all conceptions of the good; it applies only to reasonable conceptions of the good. However, this only postpones the problem, for why should we believe that the way in which we describe the concept of "reasonableness" is neutral, uncontroversial, etc?
11. Note that there are two, distinct problems that neutralists must solve: one is to argue that the right is (morally) *prior* to the good; the other is the question at hand: to defend that there is a distinction which can be adequately and neutrally defended between the right and the good in the first place.
12. Pauer-Studer mentions three different ways in which liberal neutralists can justify state coercion or "paternalism"; "...the principle of equal freedom, the principle of negative consequences, and the harm principle." (Pauer-Studer, p.185.) However, it seems to me that a more parsimonious attitude is called for, and that the harm principle can fulfil the role as a master principle, making the other two dimensions redundant.
13. ...or that B believes, or does not believe, that p; or that B prefers, or does not prefer x.

14. All this is of course radically incomplete, and does nothing much but postpone all the interesting stuff in the analysis of a plausible conception of the harm principle. But remember that I am not out to defend the harm principle; I only offer a rough and ready starting description of the gist of the harm principle with which I believe most liberals (and many other) will agree.
15. It might be the case that there is room for a non-liberal kind of neutralism that need not involve a specifically liberal interpretation of the harm principle etc. However, I know of no such theory, and I find it hard to envisage what would motivate such a proposal.
16. Some might find this puzzling. With "adequately" I intend the following: Some neutralists discard the aspiration to full theoretical neutrality and opt for a defence of N which is wholly or partially based in a, or some, conceptions(s) of the good. Hence, it seems that "any old" argument – neutral or otherwise – can play the role of justification for the practice of neutrality (at least, arguments involving conceptions of the good cannot be discarded straight away.) However, it is clear that this non-neutrality cannot be carried too far: Imagine, for instance, a conceptualisation of N in which N is defended in terms of a substantial ideal of autonomy. Now, it might be the case that something like the N follows; yet, in what sense is it that such a political regime is neutral vis-à-vis conceptions of the good. Seen from the non-autonomy endorsing citizen, the political practice will hardly seem neutral. (I cannot here undertake to elaborate this line of thought, but I hope the problems are rather evident.) Hence, "adequately" neutral means something like "not immediately involving the neutralist in contradictions or compromising the political practice of neutrality".
17. Naturally, no plausible political theory would (or could) allow perfect equality between all conceptions of the good.
18. Holtug operates with the distinction between "prudential" and "moralised" concepts of harm, see Holtug, pp. 364ff.
19. I bypass here eventual complications arising from the inclusion of animals, extraterrestrial aliens, etc., in political philosophy.
20. It might sound as if I am sailing very close to subjectivist winds here; as if I am endorsing a view on which well-being is relative to a person's endorsement of a given state of affairs. In fact, I believe that well-being is independent of endorsement (of course, endorsement generally "tracks" well-being), but I also believe that, in general, person's endorsement of a given state of affairs is a good indication of it being a positive contribution to well-being; hence, a plausible theory of well-being will "ring true" to rational and well-informed persons.
21. It might be said that republicans and communitarians are simply wrong about this last point (in fact, I am inclined to believe that they are); however, that would be a *moral* argument, and hence, it would force the move from a non-moralised concept of harm to a moralised one.
22. My intuition – excuse the vagueness of expression – is that it is possible to formulate a plausible version of an objective list or perfectionist theory of value which almost, but not entirely, bypasses this problem. But this is because attractive perfectionist theories fuse prudential and moral considerations – elements into an amalgam. See Griffin, p.63. In effect, such theories deny or transcend the right – good distinction and the distinction between prudential and moral theories. However, such theories seem eminently ill-fitted for neutralist purposes as they involve considerations of the good life as their foundation and because they are deeply controversial, at least seen from a neutralist standpoint.
23. This might sound as an absurd point to raise in the first place: how can theories of what is good for persons be independent of theories of the good? However, neutralist usage of the term "conception of the good" rarely, if ever, implies that it should include more theoretically tinged considerations such as (metaethical or axiological) theories of the good.

24. In general, neutralism rests very uneasily with consequentialist frameworks or elements. See Sher, pp. 45ff, 106ff Caney, *passim*. It might be suggested that, by adopting a highly specific theory of the good – e.g., a pluralistic conception which puts a very high premium on intrusions of the private sphere, on paternalism etc. – a consequentialist framework just might do the trick for the neutralist. This is not the place to discuss in sufficient details what can plausibly brought into a theory of the good (my attitude towards this is, in point of fact, extremely permissive); however, my intuition is that this is not a palatable route for the neutralist, because they would want their theory of the good to be as slender or "thin" and uncontroversial as possible, and any *a priori* definition of the (dis-)value of, e.g., privacy must remain highly controversial and will fail to be adequately neutral between competing, reasonable conceptions of the good.
25. Holtug puts forward a structurally similar argument against Raz' use of the harm principle, and writes in conclusion: "However, it now seems that what is doing the work [of distinguishing between relevant and irrelevant aspects of harm] is a more or less full-blown theory of justice, rather than the Harm Principle. In order to apply the Harm Principle, we need to know what people are entitled to. And in order to know what people are entitled to, we need a theory of justice." (Holtug, p. 385.)

Literature:

Caney, S. (1991) "Consequentialist Defences of Liberal Neutrality", *Philosophical Quarterly,* Vol. 41, #165
Bird, C. (1996)"Mutual Respect and Neutral Justification", *Ethics,* Vol. 107, #1
Charlesworth, M. (1993) *Bioethics in a Liberal Society* (Cambridge; Cambridge University Press)
Dworkin, R.M. (1977) *Taking Rights Seriously* (Cambridge (Mass.); Harvard University Press)
– (1985a) "Liberalism",
–(1985b) "Do We Have a Right to Pornography?",
– Both in (1985) Ronald Dworkin, *A Matter of Principle* Oxford; Oxford University Press)
– (1995) "Foundations of Liberal Equality" in Stephen Darwall (ed.), *Equal Freedom (Selected Tanner Lectures on Human Values)* (Ann Arbor; The University of Michigan Press)
Edmundson, W. (1998) *Three Anarchical Fallacies* (Cambridge;Cambridge University Press)
Griffin, J. (1986) *Well-being – Its Meaning, Measurement and Moral Importance* (Oxford; Clarendon Press)
Hart, H.L.A. (1963) *Law, Liberty, and Morality* (Stanford; Stanford University Press)
Holmes, S. (1988) "Gag rules or the Politics of Omission", in Jon Elster and Rune Slagstad (eds.) *Constitutionalism and Democracy* (Cambridge; Cambridge University Press)
Holtug, N. (2002) "The Harm Principle", *Ethical Theory and Moral Practice* #5
Hurka, T. (1993) *Perfectionism* (Oxford, Oxford University Press)
Kagan, S. (1998) *Normative Ethics* (Boulder; Westview Press)
Kymlicka, W. (1990) *Contemporary Political Philosophy* (Oxford; Clarendon Press)
Mendus, S. (1989) *Toleration and the Limits of Liberalism* (London; Macmillan)
Neal, P. (1997) *Liberalism and its Discontents* (London; Macmillan)
Nielsen, M.E.J. (2003) "On Behalf of Perfectionism: A Reply to Pauer-Studer", *Philosophical Explorations* 6 (1)
Pauer-Studer, H. (2001) "Liberalism, Perfectionism, and Civic Virtue", *Philosophical Explorations,* vol. IV, #3
Rawls, J. (1971) *A Theory of Justice* (Oxford; Oxford University Press)
– (1993) *Political Liberalism* (New York; Colombia University Press)

– (2001) *Justice as Fairness – A Restatement* (Cambridge (Mass.); Belknap/Harvard)
Raz, J. (1986) *The Morality of Freedom* (Oxford; Oxford University Press)
– (1994) "Facing Diversity: The Case of Epistemic Abstinence", in Raz, *Ethics in the Public Domain* (Oxford; Clarendon Press)
Sher, G. (1997) *Beyond Neutrality* (Cambridge; Cambridge University Press)
Wall, S. (1998) *Liberalism, Perfectionism and Restraint* (Cambridge; Cambridge University Press)

FORESIGHT AND BLAMEWORTHINESS FOR ACTION CONSEQUENCES

NIKOLAJ NOTTELMANN

Department of Media, Cognition, and Communication
Division of Philosophy
Njalsgade 80
2300 Copenhagen S
e-mail: nottelmn@hum.ku.dk

I. Introduktion

It seems obvious that the notions of foresight and moral blameworthiness for action consequences are intimately related. E.g. it may be held that an agent is excused for whatever consequences follow from her conduct, if it was impossible for her to foresee those consequences up until their time of occurrence. In other words the following principle may be submitted:

(F) If an agent A could not possibly have foreseen a consequence C of her actions or omissions, A is not morally blameworthy for the occurrence of C, no matter the further circumstances.[1]

In the present paper I shall scrutinize the notion of foresight relevant to the deontic evaluation of action or omission consequences. I shall argue that (F) does not hold, but may plausibly be replaced by a weaker principle.

II. Michael Zimmermann's definition of foresight

The exact sense of foresight involved in principles like (F) has not been given much attention in the literature. In fact, recent authors treating on the relation between foresight and moral blameworthiness for action or omission consequences have generally been less than willing to explicate the notion of foresight involved in their considerations.[2] Michael Zimmermann, being an exception to this rule, has proposed the following definition:

> P foresees at $t1$ (to some degree) that e [an event] will occur at $t2$ if and only P occurrently believes at $t1$ that (there is some probability that) e will occur at $t2$ [where $t1$ is earlier than $t2$].[3]

We may begin by noticing two peculiarities in Zimmermann's definition. One concerns his "to some degree" qualification. Presumably, this qualification is supposed to correspond to the second parenthesis, such that, according to Zimmermann, an agent foresees to a 60% degree that an event will happen tomorrow if, and only if, she consciously believes that there is a 60% probability that that event will happen tomorrow. However, this seems a slightly unnatural way of expressing the latter proposition. If the agent has this belief, it arguably seems more natural to say that she simply *foresees* that the event will happen than to say that she foresees it to any limited degree: After all, she believes that the event is more likely to happen than not. I shall therefore prefer to leave out the strange "to some degree" qualification in my preferred conception of foresight.

Also it would seem that, on the most natural understanding of foresight, if I foresee that an occurrence will occur, I simply take it to be more likely than not that this occurrence will occur, i.e. that it is more than 50% probable that the occurrence will occur within a designated time-interval. In contrast, if I take it to be less likely that an occurrence will occur than not occur (e.g. if, on Zimmermann's definition, I "foresaw" it to a 40% degree), it seems odd to say, if it occurred, that I nevertheless foresaw it: If I believed it only 40% likely that my home town football team would win the championship and it won nonetheless, I am hardly entitled to say that I foresaw this outcome. Thus the notion defined by Zimmermann is not exactly a standard notion of foresight. For reasons that shall soon emerge I shall go along with the basics of it nevertheless.

However, some crucial modifications must still be made. Firstly, there are some terminological problems. We may clearly be blamed for action or omission consequences, which do not qualify as events in a colloquial sense, but are rather states of some kind. E.g. I may blame you for my present headache, since yesterday you urged me drink yet another bottle of beer. I will therefore prefer the more neutral term "occurrence" to Zimmermann's "event". Also I will allow that "t2" might be a(n) (open-ended) time-interval such as "next year" or "the future": Clearly it does not matter to an agent's blameworthiness for some action consequence whether she foresaw its exact temporal location.

III. Belief and acceptance

The most basic problem inherent in Zimmermann's definition of foresight arguably concerns the doxastic attitude involved. I shall maintain that belief, traditionally understood, is not the relevant type of attitude in the context of the deontic evaluation of action consequences, and should be replaced with a notion of acceptance, properly understood. Jonathan L Cohen has offered the following definition of acceptance:

> But in my sense to accept that p is to have or adopt a policy of deeming, position or postulating that p – that is of going along with that proposition (either for the long term or for immediate purposes only) as a premise in some or all contexts for one's own or other' proofs, argumentations, inferences, deliberations, etc. whether or not one assents and whether or not one feels it to be true that p.[4]

Belief that p on the other hand, as this attitude has traditionally been understood, involves a degree of conviction that p is true. In Wilfrid Sellars' words "in a certain sense the believer takes it for granted, regards it as already settled, as not a matter of debate or of internal puzzlement that"[5] the proposition believed is true.

Accepting that p in Cohen's sense clearly does neither require one to believe that p in the above sense, nor to form the belief that p in the future: One can go along with a proposition, without being in the least convinced that it is true. If e.g. I am doctor needing to administer a treatment in an urgent situation, I may well decide to act on the premise that a certain treatment is salient (rather than doing nothing at all), even if I have no clue as to its actual efficacy.

To see that it is acceptance rather than belief, which is the key attitude involved in foresight of the relevant kind, regard the following example: Consider again the case of a doctor, this time a compulsively sceptical specimen. At a certain time, this doctor must administer a drug to a seriously wounded patient. She is aware that she is expected to administer this drug. Still, due to her sceptical disposition she does not really believe that the drug will help the patient. In fact, it is impossible for her to believe that her failure to administer the drug will affect the patient's future at all. She does not administer the drug. As a result of her omission the patient dies.

Now, even if it was indeed impossible for the doctor to believe that anything bad would result from her omission, does this fact acquit her of moral blameworthiness for the patient's death? I think this is highly implausible, if we assume that it was indeed possible for the doctor to *accept* that the patient would be harmed as a consequence of her omission, i.e. that it was possible for her to *act on the assumption* that the patient would be harmed, even if she could not believe that proposition. In fact, in the example given, it may well be that the doctor *should* have acted on this assumption, despite her sceptical disposition.

In the light of the above example, it seems clear that an agent's ability to form beliefs about the consequences of her actions or omissions is only relevant to a deontic evaluation of the consequences of those actions or omissions, insofar as those beliefs matter to her conduct. If unforeseeability of any kind is to excuse her even partially from moral blame for undesirable consequences of her conduct, the crucial point must be whether it was impossible for her to act on certain assumptions regarding the future, i.e. whether it was impossible for her to accept certain propositions regarding the future. I shall thus be satisfied to submit that acceptance (in Cohen's sense) is the type of doxastic attitude relevant to deontic evaluations of action consequences based on foresight.

IV. Increase in risk

There is also an issue concerning the "non-zero probability" involved in Zimmermann's account that must be resolved if the resulting notion of foresight is going to be relevant to a deontological context. It might seem that there are probabilities so small that we are entitled to ignore them in our practical reasoning, in the sense that we cannot be blamed for any undesirable consequences of an action or omission, even if, in performing them, we accepted that such a small risk obtained. Remember that, on reflection, we must acknowledge that there is a tiny chance that somebody will die or get hurt from almost anything we do.

Imagine, for instance, that I bow down to tie my shoelaces. Further, imagine that in bowing down I accept that, as a result of my bowing down, I might by an incredible misfortune move the surrounding air in a way that ultimately brings about a lethal thundercloud on the other side of the globe, killing hundreds of people in Australia.[6] Suppose now that as a result of my bowing down to tie my shoelaces, disastrous consequences of this type do in fact result. Still, does my foresight that by bowing down I might kill hundreds of people in Australia make me one bit less excused for those deaths. Hardly!

However, examples like the above do not really point to a level of risk that I am entitled to ignore as insignificant to my actions or omissions. In the above case, a tiny risk *also* obtained that some great harm would result from my *not* bowing down to tie my shoelaces. In fact then, no obvious *increase* in the risk of a thundercloud in Australia resulted from my bowing down. However, if the risks adhering to the performance or omission of an action are not balanced in this way, things look differently:

Imagine e.g. that a canned soup manufacturer accepted that there was a very tiny increase (say 0.00001) in the risk that someone would die as a result of ingesting his soup, once he added a specific cheapening ingredient to it, and that an increase in such a risk actually obtained. He nevertheless went on to add the ingredient. Now, if someone actually died as a result of eating the soup, certainly it seems wrong to acquit the soup manufacturer on the grounds that he only accepted a *very tiny* increase in the risk of this undesirable outcome. This example points to the fact that it is acceptances of an *increase* in risk, rather than an acceptance of risk proper that matter to the deontic evaluation of action consequences and that even an acceptance of a tiny increase in risk may forfeit an unforeseeability excuse.

Before stating my definition yet a further crucial observation is required: In order to be of relevance to a principle like (F) the acceptance of an increase in risk must relate narrowly to the agent's action. In our example of the sceptical doctor, she might clearly still offer an appropriate unforeseeability excuse, even if, when the patient was in her care, she did in fact accept that the risk that the patient would die was continuously increasing. What matters, is clearly which increases in risk she accepted or was able to accept *as resulting from her actions or omissions*. Perhaps, it was simply impossible for her to accept at the relevant time that her administration of the relevant drug in the least affected the patient's chances of survival, even if she accepted that those chances were continuously dwindling. If so, her unforeseeability excuse appears strong.

V. Defining foresight

Following the remarks on Zimmermann's definition, we may opt for the following definition of foresight as the one relevant to the moral evaluation of action consequences:

> (Foresight): An agent A *foresees* at t that, given her performance of a certain action or omission C, the occurrence o will occur in the time-interval T, if, and only if, A accepts at t that, if she performs C, *as a consequence of* her performance of C the risk increases that o will occur within T. Here, no point of time falling within T is earlier than t.

On this understanding of foresight an action or omission consequence is *unforeseeable*, if, and only if, at the time of action or omission the relevant agent could not possibly accept that an increase in the risk of this consequence resulted from her action or omission.

It would seem that this definition takes us close to an understanding of unforeseeability vindicating (F): If a ball-throwing youngster is somehow fundamentally barred from including in his practical reasoning the premise that the windows of his neighbourhood are more likely to be broken when he throws his ball at them, it seems plausible that we should excuse him for the damage he inflicts on our windows, no matter our annoyance: In a crucial sense, the actual consequences of his action are simply beyond the horizon of his practical reasoning.

However, I shall argue below, (F) is not home free.

VI. Excusability and relevant foresight

Regard again the example of the canned soup manufacturer. Now assume that, at the time he added the cheapening ingredient to his soup, the occurrence that some people would die was *unforeseeable* in the sense given above: The soup manufacturer could not possibly act on the assumption that, as a result of his adding the cheapening ingredient to the soup, an increase in risk obtained that soup consumers would die. Nevertheless, while adding the ingredient the soup manufacturer *did* accept that, as a result of his adding the ingredient, an increase in risk obtained that his consumers would get severely ill and even paralysed.

Here it seems plausible that, even if the consumer deaths were unforeseeable for the soup manufacturer, he is still not excused for them. On the other hand, if, at the time he added the ingredient, the manufacturer could not possible foresee that, given his adding the ingredient to the soup, severe bodily harm would occur, but could in fact foresee that some mild harm would occur, e.g. an occasional mild headache in an addicted consumer, an unforeseeability excuse still seems in place.

The above example points to the conclusion that unforeseeability cannot act as an all-out excuse. Even if an agent could not possibly foresee the actual consequences of her action, she is still not excused from blame for them. Only, it may seem, if she could not possibly foresee consequences of a relevant *degree of undesirability*, she remains excused. In the example above, severe bodily harm appeared to be of a relevant degree of undesirability relative to death: If the manufacturer could have foreseen that severe bodily harm would occur from his action, it does not seem to excuse him that he could not possibly have foreseen that customers would actually die. On the other hand, a mild degree of bodily harm, such as a headache, plausibly was not of the right degree. Even if the manufacturer could foresee that a few headaches would occur, he might still appropriately excuse himself from the death of a customer on the basis that he could not possibly have foreseen it.

However, even if an agent did in fact foresee consequences even *worse* than the actual consequences of her action, plausibly an unforeseeability excuse might still be appropriate. Consider the following example: Adam is a person highly oblivious to the needs of others. Some day he arrives at the local parking lot and observes that no parking space is vacant except a bay reserved for a disabled woman. Adam parks his car in the reserved bay, accepting the proposition that in the near future this will mean a terrible problem for the disabled woman. In fact, Adam foresees that the woman will be unable to get her medication in time and will suffer terribly as a result. Now, as a result of Adam's parking his car in the reserved spot, a prowling burglar is able to hide behind his car, and does not get spotted by a police patrol, as she would otherwise have been. Here, I take it, even though Adam did in fact foresee far worse consequences of his action, he is not to blame for the consequence that the burglar did not get caught, if he could not possibly have foreseen that his action of parking the car would beget a consequence of that kind.

The above considerations point to the conclusion that an unforeseeability excuse is only appropriate when the agent could not have foreseen consequences of a relevant degree of undesirability *related* in a relevant way to the actual action consequence under deontic evaluation. The principle (F) should be replaced with

> (F*) If an agent A could not possibly have foreseen a consequence C of her actions or omissions and could not possibly have foreseen any consequence C* of her actions or omissions, C* being of a relevant degree of undesirability and relevantly related to C, A is not morally blameworthy for the occurrence of C, no matter the further circumstances

In the examples above the soup manufacturer's foresight that soup consumer would get severely hurt, appeared to be relevantly related to the actual consequence that soup consumers were killed. On the other hand, Adam's foresight that the disabled woman would suffer badly was not in any relevant way related to the actual consequence that the burglar went free.

In general, though, it is not easy to see how measures of relevance in the context of F* may be calculated. Even given full knowledge of an agent's doxastic condition up until the occurrence of some consequence of her conduct, determining the appropriateness of an unforeseeability excuse from moral blameworthiness for that consequence remains a fuzzy matter.

Notes

1. Justin Oakley & Dean Cocking has it that "According to a widely-accepted account, the concept of moral responsibility involves two conditions; avoidability and foreseeability. That is, I am morally responsible for consequences C if, and only if, they are among the foreseeable results of what I could reasonably have avoided doing". Oakley & Cocking 1994, 205-206. Insofar as blameworthiness depends on responsibility and omissions qualify as doings, this principle entails (F).
2. In fact the literature on the deontological relevance of foresight has been almost singularly obsessed with the relation between foresight and intention. See e.g. Baldwin 1979 and Aulisio 1996.
3. Zimmermann 1986, 206.
4. Cohen 1989, 368. It should be noted that in the epistemological literature the term 'acceptance' has been used in a number of alternative senses. E.g. William Alston have tied the term "acceptance" much closer to belief: "I understand "accepting" a proposition as an activity that gives rise to a belief." Alston 1989, 121. Mark Kaplan has submitted that "X accepts p" is just shorthand for "X would defend P were her sole aim to defend the truth". Kaplan 1981, 138. Robert Stalnaker has used "acceptance" as a generic notion, treating belief as one among several "acceptance concepts" Stalnaker 2002, 159. Whatever the legitimacy of these alternative uses, they do not comply with the present.
5. Sellars 1989, 128.
6. I assume that this is possible on a folksy version of the physics of chaotic systems having it that a butterfly flapping its wings in South America may cause a storm in Australia.

Literature

Alston, William P. 1989. *Epistemic Justification. Essays in the Theory of Knowledge*. London: Cornell University Press.
Aulisio, Mark P. 1996. On the Importance of the Intention/Foresight Distinction. *American Catholic Philosophical Quarterly* 70: 189-205.
Baldwin, Thomas: 1979. Foresight and Responsibility. *Philosophy* 54: 347-360.
Cohen, L. Jonathan. 1989. Belief and Acceptance. *Mind* 98: 367-389.
Kaplan, Mark. 1981. Rational Acceptance. *Philosophical Studies* 40: 129-145.
Oakley, Justin & Cocking, Dean. 1994. Consequentialism, Moral Responsibility, and the Intention/Foresight Distinction. *Utilitas* 6: 201-216.
Sellars, Wilfrid: 1989. *The Metaphysics of Epistemology. Lectures by Wilfrid Sellars*. Atascadero: Ridgeview.
Stalnaker, Robert. 2002. Epistemic Consequentialism II. *Proceedings of the Aristotelian Society, Supplementary Volume* 76: 153-168.
Zimmermann, Michael J. 1986. Negligence and Moral Responsibility. *Nous* 20: 199-218.

REALITY CONFOUNDED: DISCUSSION REVIEW

STIG ALSTRUP RASMUSSEN

Department of Media, Cognition, and Communication
Division of Philosophy
Njalsgade 80
2300 Copenhagen S

Søren Harnow Klausen, *Reality Lost and Found: An Essay on the Realism-Antirealism Controversy*, Doctoral Thesis (Habilitation), University of Southern Denmark, University Press of Southern Denmark, Odense 2004; 573 pp.

By any reasonable standards, Klausen's study of the multifarious controversies between realism and anti-realists of various ilk is massive, rich and impressive, in scope as well as bulk. Both of the 'routine', main European philosophical traditions are considered, along with a good deal of historical material. There is even an attempt to seriously interface with a few other brands of academic study, at various stages in the argument. The result is not just a 'synoptic and synthetic' work (p.1); it has the air of being, at times, unduly eclectic: a volume which is somewhat uneven, yet very useful. But let us look.

Overall, the author strives to defend 'metaphysical realism', and its sequels, from the onslaughts of any party he deems fit to regard as anti-realist. The former view is to the effect that reality exists independently of human cognition, language, culture, history, practice, and what have we. Klausen regards this, very general, characterisation as the one that captures what the realist is out to make good. So there is Absolute Reality, in a, possibly extended, Lockean version. He thinks various semantical and epistemological doctrines tend to follow from this. Moreover, they follow *distinctively* from the realist conception in at least some cases, and are therefore not available to the anti-realist. Also, the scope of defensible realism is fairly comprehensive: ordinary middle-sized physical objects, the theoretical objects of microphysics, other minds, the past, and possibly more. The world is pretty much as an educated Westerner would conceive of it, independently of our possibilities of conceiving. We are, as Klausen would have it, all Aristotelians (p. 36). We believe in the independent existence of individual substances, properties, and even facts, although the latter allegedly add nothing to ontology. Furthermore, we are, despite the independent existence of all this stuff, capable of acknowledging the existence of it. So, epistemological optimism is part of Klausen's definition of 'realism'. The central Kantian enigma is in the offing; but let's follow the ways in which one may, according to Klausen, fall short of qualifying as a card-carrying realist. One may opt for

1) Subjective idealism, say Berkeley minus God.
2) Objective idealism.
3) Eliminativism.
4) Logical Positivism.
5) Relativism, however based (including social constructivism).
6) Scepticism.
7) Transcendental positions, in a fairly broad sense of 'transcendental'.
8) Epistemological Internalism.
9) Refusing to endorse the general applicability of the principle of bivalence to all meaningful sentences.

The list could probably be extended. For the time being, notice that, according to Klausen, anybody who endorses just one of (1) though (9) is a deviant from realism, hence an anti-realist.

We should grant (1) through (3), although questions do arise concerning both (2) and (3). Look at (4), however. The Logical Positivists were not, on the face of things, 'idealists'. Their core doctrine was to the effect that a declarative sentence has cognitive meaning to the extent that we know how to decide which truth value it has. Since a wide range of sentences are not guaranteed to have associated with them a procedure that would decide them, these are not cognitively meaningful. So, large tracts of theology, metaphysics, moral philosophy, aesthestics, etc., are on a par with Shostakovich's 3rd String Quartet. But this has little to do with the realism/anti-realism issue. The latter must be to do with whether or not mind-independent reality is capable of bestowing truth-values on our cognitively significant sentences. However, we gather this much, concerning Klausen: apparently anybody who denies that sentences customarily believed to be truth-apt are at all cognitively significant, is to be counted as an anti-realist. I would suggest that the contender in question is better classified as a non-cognitivist with respect to the sentences in question. Perhaps Klausen ought to agree with the logical positivist on this point. He, too, refuses seriously to countenance, e.g., the existence of moral facts. This is not because they are mind-dependent: they are not there, simply.

Now Klausen's conception of realism is rather embracing: the realist doctrine is supposed to involve endorsing not only common-sense realism, but realism with respect to 'theoretical entities' (atoms, quarks, genes, etc), as well. It is true, of course, that the Logical Positivists tended to take a dim view as to the independent existence of the latter in particular. As Klausen defines 'realism', we must therefore allow that they were, to a varying degree, anti-realists. On the other hand, Klausen himself fails to seriously address the tangled issue of how to combine common-sense realism with realism in respect of quantum reality. In the famous example: my desk consists, from the latter point of view, mostly of empty space, whereas, on the former, it is a solid mass resulting from careful carpentry. So, is it mind-independently one or the other? Both? Neither? This question bears on eliminativism (3), too. The salient point is however this: we begin to suspect that Klausen's definition of 'realism' is perhaps too inclusive for comfort. Our suspicion is borne out as we move along.

Let us approach the matter thus: Klausen considers that there are broadly two kinds of argument in support of realism. (I) Trancendental arguments and (II) empirical, or naturalistic, ones. The latter are at least mildly question-begging, however; and the former seem to rely on an anti-realist premiss. The grounds for staying with realism then derive from 'metaepistemological' considerations, the idea of which is that 'it is rational for us stick to our realist beliefs' (p.7). What makes realism our best bet turns out to be an application of the argument to the best explanation of phenomena, as they present themselves to the enquiring and attentive mind, combined with the view that we are all pre-theoretic realists, anyway. I agree with much of what Klausen puts forth in support of these theses. There is, however, a question as to whether the transcendental philosopher really is best seen as a straightforward anti-realist. He is, if we adopt Klausen's definition of 'realism'. Also, Kant's famous proof of the existence of the external world supports no more than the conclusion than the world, considered as our organised experience, exists. A similar point holds for later efforts by, *inter alia*, John McDowell [McDowell 1994/1996]. However, Kant's overall philosophy was well characterised by Strawson as an uneasy compromise between realism and idealism (anti-realism) [Strawson 1966]. Klausen's framework leaves no scope for such subtleties.

Furthermore, it is not at all clear that the realist has the advantage over the anti-realist when it comes to 'infer' to the best explanation of phenomena. At least, this does not seem obvious in general. Why is this a PC before me? The obvious reason seems to be that there is one, and observational circumstances are right. But most 'anti-realists' would not deny this. They would contend, rather, with what is the import of that statement. Could it not be, e.g., that the PC really consists of elementary particles suitable interacting in empty space? Or might not my PC be an emanation of the Godhead? Or do I have to think of it as an object that would be there, even if the fact that this was so was possibly verification-transcendent? The second suggestion could probably be ruled out as not the best available explanation, overall. But the first case is at least doubtful, and the third raises the question as to how we could even aim at explaining phenomena by possibly in principle verification-transcendent facts. How could we aim at establishing their existence? And even if we could, how might invoking them extend the explanatory powers of our theories?

There is an antecedent worry about Klausen's terminology. His official doctrine of realism is captured by his (R3) – or, to his mind equivalently, (R4). Here is (R3) (p. 22):

> "Realism is the view that the world exists and has its fundamental properties independently of the way it is experienced, spoken or written about or coped with by conscious beings..."

Further clauses aim to deal with minds, be they mine or other's. Other minds exist, apparently, independently of our epistemic endeavours. Common-sense realism tells us as much. My own mental states exist only mind-dependently, because it is commonly known that *esse* equals *percipi* in my own case (p. 14). One might quarrel with the latter; but let sleeping dogs lie (A huge dog, in this case). It is obvious that Klausen conflates several issues. His aim is to characterise and defend 'robust' realism. This is partly realist, partly robust (a 'package deal', e.g., p. 6). Also, it has to be right that realism with respect to very little is not worthy of its name. But Klausen fails to realise that 'realism' is not an absolute term, but a relative one: we are realists, or not, *about* certain areas of reality. Therefore and despite sustained efforts, he does not tell us what realism is. Instead, we are being told quite a lot of that about which we should be realists. Furthermore, inherent in Klausen's thought about realism is the idea that a realist must be an epistemological optimist. Reality is there, mind-independently. However, we mostly get it right when attempting to establish what reality is like. But why is this not little short of a miracle, if it is true? Which is perhaps why this doctrine is not particularly to the liking of anybody with substantial realist leanings. Also, thinking about this kind of problem constitutes the reasoning that turned Kant towards transcendental idealism.

Concerning (9), Klausen insists that certain semantical ideas are 'essential' to the realist doctrine. They are however not 'constitutive' (e.g., p. 39). Following Michael Devitt [Devitt 1984], he argues that

> *"...one can hardly make a semantic thesis constitutive of realism and at the same time maintain that realism requires that there be no significant connection between reality and conceptual and linguistic matters."*

Despite of its provenance, this sort of statement simply harbours a blatant confusion. It is true that language, along with genuine conceptual thought, was generated by one species among many inhabiting a tiny speck in the Universe. But nobody claims that we, or our language, created the Universe. The claim is, rather, that we have no other access to the Universe than through our conceptualizations of bits and pieces of it. The anti-realist's point is that, for that very reason, sentences utilizing conceptual means not at our disposal must be devoid of truth value. Also, one may wonder about the distinction between essential and constitutive. If it is constitutive to being a hippopotamus that it be a quadruped, then having this property must be essential as well. The converse implication may perhaps be a moot point. I suspect the matter boils down to entailment not being symmetrical: fully fledged realism entails general adherence to the principle of bivalence, but the converse entailment fails. Or so Klausen would have it.

To make matters definite, consider Michael Dummett's view: the realist endorses, while the anti-realist refuses to embrace, the general applicability of the principle of bivalence to sentences of the kind under consideration, irrespective of our current warrant for issuing a guarantee that we shall ever be in a position to decide which truth-values the sentences severally possess [Rasmussen & Ravnkilde 1982; Rasmussen 1990]. The definition of 'realism' contained in this statement does not, *pace* Devitt and Klausen, involve detracting from the realist's belief in the independent existence of the relevant chunks of reality. On the contrary: if reality is such as to make either definitely true or definitely not-true the statement that Alexander the Great had pimples at his 13th birthday, then the statement has a truth-value not dependent on our ability to establish which one it has. It is true, of course, that the relevant truth-making fact is conceptualized by us. But something similar is bound to happen, no matter how 'realism' is defined. This does not tend to diminish the purported ontological independence of the fact to somebody sharing Klausen's fact-realistic leanings. At least, this ought to be treated as a separate issue, as a question about the status of facts.

The quotation above vividly illustrates a fairly widespread mistake. It is thought that reality must be independent of language, as reality was there long before any cognizant being appeared. Therefore, nothing to do with mind and language can enter into the definition of realism. The premiss is incontestable, certainly to a realist. Also, it ought to be pointed out, to any reasonable brand of anti-realist. The inference is however a failure. It is we who define 'realism'. If the radical realist is right, the definition does not even indirectly have much bearing on the way reality is. It is still our definition, neither more nor – more significantly – less.

Is there not a hint, here, of a confusion of definitions of, respectively, 'reality' and 'realism'? The former is best characterised in ground-floor linguistic terms. The latter, however, just might be best depicted at the reflective, meta-linguistic level.

In the light of the above, (6) seems completely out of place. The sceptic must be somebody who thinks that reality seriously outstrips our capacities for knowing, even in principle. He is therefore a natural born realist, not an anti-realist. Klausen's confusion on this point is, first, not absolutely thoroughgoing; and second, has some support in the vast literature on the subject; but is, third, nevertheless indicative of his general running together of epistemological and ontological issues. Generally: the more realist one is, the more prone one is to fall prey to (Cartesian) scepticism. This is not to deny that even the anti-realist in respect of some areas of discourse may be vulnerable to a milder brand of scepticism. This might well happen, whenever the kind of truth (falsity) for which sentences pertaining to the discourse are apt is non-monotonous (because of defeasibility, say). The general point still stands, however.

Concerning (8), there is no doubt that epistemological externalism, as opposed to internalism, is often supposed to be the preserve of the realist. And conversely, the adoption of epistemological internalism is often supposed to bring anti-realism in its train. Klausen seems to more or less agree with this view. So that if we adopt a conception of knowledge akin to those of Goldman or Nozick, we must be realists. However, this view is wholly mistaken. It is perfectly possible to endorse, say, Nozick's tracking conditions while being an anti-realist [Nozick 1981]. Why should Husserl not do so, for instance? (I take Husserl to be a transcendental idealist, hence an anti-realist.) If one believes otherwise, we have a case of ontological question-begging in a big way. The crux of the matter is, in this case, how to separate the issue of knowledge attibutions from that of individuating contents of propositional attitudes.

Subjective idealism (1) is the view that everything is what it looks like – no more, no less. It is perhaps easier to remember the 'no more'-bit than the other part. Hence we encounter all sorts of, e.g., phenomenalistic kinds of reductionism. These never worked, as Klausen is well aware. However, perhaps this is easy thrift. Non-reductionist anti-realism of the Wittgensteinian/Dummettian kind could still be in play [Dummett 1963]. Objective idealism (2) is not really distinguishable from realism. It is a doctrine as to what Absolute Reality is. Let it be Spirit. We do not, if we are sane, believe this; but it does not matter to any human, or other, concern.

Which raises a further question: why should it matter to anybody whether realism or anti-realism wins the day? Klausen seems to think that there is no need to answer this question. Perhaps he even considers it slightly absurd. Dummett, Wright, and others have thought important the question as to why we should care. One reason is that while a Dummettian realist has a right to adopt classical logic, along with all reasoning patterns that go with it, the anti-realist does not. The impact on the practice of doing mathematics is dramatic [Dummett 1973]. However, the repercussions extend to other areas as well. Klausen takes care to avoid serious consideration of issues that might embroil him in questions of this kind. This is fair enough; but why, then, should it bother me at all if a convincing case were to made that the world is the expression of will and representation?

There is a further serious question involved. The reason why Klausen is unconcerned with the consequences of adopting anti-realism, rather than realism, is that he concentrates on (I):

(I) Is mind, language, etc., *constitutive* of physical reality, be it micro or macro?

From this point of view, it does appear to matter whether my desk consists of Spirit, or whatever, even if holding on to this aberration has no consequences whatever for anything I might do or say at the level of ground-floor performance. Also, semantical considerations will appear, at best, as a side-issue. On the Dummett/Wright view, the pertinent question is however (II):

(II) Can there be more to physical reality than is in principle ascertainable by the attentive and enquiring human mind?

That is, could truths about physical reality be possibly verification-trancendent? Now semantical issues cannot be isolated and relegated to a perfunctory discussion (Chapter 2). They are crucial. Furthermore, they now have a direct bearing on our comportment outside academic philosophy.

The issue arising over relativism (5) is dicey to place within the pattern of the other ongoing controversies. Klausen comes down on the side that we are dealing with a version, or versions, of anti-realism. This might seem plausible, in view of the fact that, according to any decent brand of relativism, the world is dependent on whatever apparatus humans can bring to bear, cognitive or otherwise. However, matters are not that simple. An ontological relativist will argue roughly as follows:

(a) Significant variability: Relative to some parameter (culture, language, class, race, gender, etc.), we disagree over the truth value of some crucial propositions.
(b) We cannot, in principle, decide the issue, collectively.
(c) Anti-realism: If a decision as between p and not-p is in principle impossible, there is no truth of the matter.
(d) So: propositions p and not-p are equally good.

There might be several objections to the above train of thought. Klausen – to my mind quite rightly – takes issue with (a). In crucial respects cognizant beings agree about more than meets the eye.

However, he comes up with things like the following (p. 6):

> "There are clear traces of antirealism in ancient Indian and Greek philosophy, as well as in many of the early Renaissance thinkers. And the view has many different sources.The process of enlightenment and modernisation, the voyages of discovery, the propagation of new political and moral ideals, social crises and the development of new information technologies are all factors which have prompted the formation of antirealist ideas."

Most of this is hard to fathom. However, to the extent that we can put a charitable interpretation on these words, they tend to support premiss (a) – which Klausen generally does not endorse. This is as good a place as anywhere to lodge a complaint against the above kind of generalised statement. Even Klausen must admit that ancient Indians, Captain Cook, and Bill Gates probably have humanity in common; but that is about it. The thing about the great voyages was that Europeans discovered the existence of different sets of *mores* around the Globe. And these perceptions were of course to some extent right. None of this even tends towards anti-realism. In this kind of case, relativism – if that is anti-realism – is not close. If anything, there might be support for premiss (a).

Also, Klausen ought to have been challenging (c), or the move to (d), as he is engaged in philosophical enquiry, rather than anthropological or historical studies. A very difficult question remains, however: is an avowedly internal realist really a kind of anti-realist? In general, how does relativism relate to anti-realism?

There are several issues involved. To the Dummettian, realism and anti-realism can arise, as an issue, only over fairly clear-cut chunks of reality, as described by declarative sentences pertaining to a fixed language, some of which are such that we cannot now guarantee to ever be in a position to decide their several truth-values. If sentences do not enjoy guaranteed truth-values, on whatever standards are in play, they are Dummettian problematic sentences. However, the relativist normally engages at a different point of attack. He will, typically, ignore the Dummettian issue and point, instead, to differing standards of proof, evidence, etc. – generally: epistemological standards or possibly sensibilities. It is quite possible that various (groups of) people really have differing standards. However this would tend to support premiss (a) in the above.

To confuse us even further, (a) makes little sense unless people can have genuinely different opinions as to a definite proposition, p. But the content of p has to be stable, across the relevant differences among the tribes involved. However, if standards of evidence differ, how are we to ensure that there is genuine disagreement as to the same propositional content? Famously, Davidson – to some extent following Quine – has presented grounds for assuming that we really can disagree, on the basis of wideranging, significant agreement. However, his argument has an anti-realist flavour to it. Also, his line of argument tends to undercut (a) – (b). It amounts, then, to an anti-realist argument that the issue of relativism cannot be too serious [Davidson 1974].

The upshot seems to be that Klausen is right that radical relativism relies on an anti-realist premiss, and to that extent may be counted as a form of anti-realism. But less radical versions of relativism concern epistemological issues mainly, or differing sensibilities as between varying tribes of humans. The entire emphasis is on (a) and (b). The conclusion often is a kind of scepticism: there is a fact of the matter, but we are debarred from telling which one it is. Or the conclusion might be along the lines of the impossibility of debating over matters of 'taste', possibly generalised to suit the target area. In short, the proper response to a particular brand of relativism is highly sensitive to the exact circumstances of the challenge.

Klausen's definition of realism is a multiple hybrid. First, ontology is mingled with optimistic epistemology. That is why the sceptic is, by definition, relegated to the dungeons of anti-realism. Second, the *shape* of realist doctrine is not distinguished from the *substance* of the doctrine. So, if one is not 'robustly' realist, one is not a realist at all. Robustness seems to shackle its adherent to the mind- and language-independence of more ultimate furniture of the universe than he might find himself comfortable with. There are, of course, things big and small. Their properties also enjoy mind-independent existence. Facts are in, as well. I think there is an issue here: the *scope* of ones realism, on the one hand, and the *depth* of ones realism, on the other.

Quite generally, I should go along with the mind-independence of properties, if I bought that of facts. But I do not. Facts are (perhaps some refinement of) true propositions. Facts, then, are abstract objects. So are properties, since these are the residue from dropping whatever you may think is attached to namelike expressions from propositions. Yet, Klausen seems to think that properties are causally efficacious. The quandary for Klausen is how properties can possess causal powers, since he does not want no go Australian and make properties concrete – perhaps in the manner of Armstrong [Armstrong 1997]. At least since Kant – Leibniz even – the hallmark of the concrete has been taken to be that it occurs in space and time, and is capable of causal interaction with other concrete entities. In contradistinction to these entities, *abstracta* are supposed to be causally inert [Lowe 2002, Ch. 20].

We must conclude that Klausen does not object to the mind-independent existence of abstract objects. If so, however, the next point must be that one sorely misses a discussion of these in his volume. If there are abstract properties, why is the author reticent about the possibly mind-independent existence of sets, numbers, functions, functionals, etc. The intention is not to blame Klausen for not having written another book than the admirable one he did produce. I should, however, like to know why the mind-independent existence of sets is moot, while that of abstract properties is not. The difference is probably to do with causal efficacy. Sets cannot drive anybody crazy, although attempting to understand set theory may. Similarly, I would hazard, the smell of roses in general cannot cause me to think of my wife. But the (concrete) realisation of the smell of some particular collection of roses might. And so, we are perhaps both more Australian and Aristotelian than Klausen suspects, when it comes to our thinking about properties of physical things. There are well known difficulties with this doctrine (essentially, nominalism); but these ought to be faced rather than evaded.

At least in part because of Klausen's failure to distinguish between the scope and the depth of any particular kind of realism, he comes forth with largely irrelevant, and to some extent nonsensical, statements about the supervenience of the mental on the physical. It is all summed up beautifully in the following passage (pp. 25-26):

> "The crucial point here is that none of the various concepts of supervenience entails that the mental is somehow *constitutive* of the physical. The mental does not affect the physical in any significant way. So realism is fully compatible with the supervenience of the mental."

Yes, of course realism with respect to the physical, the mental, or both is compatible with the doctrine that the mental supervenes on the physical. Why should anyone think there is a problem for the realist, even remotely? Part of the answer is that, occasionally, Klausen seems to turn his supervenience implications the wrong way around. The doctrine of supervenience is a way of non-reductively ensuring the dependence of the mental of the physical. The question of the mental being constitutive of the physical fails to arise. It would have to be the other way around, if there is a problem. In general, Klausen's grip on the notion of supervenience seems to be at best slippery – witness his statement that it is not meant to capture 'strict identity' (p. 25). I daresay. This view must be *de rigueur*.

Another worry is as follows. Klausen takes great pains to define precisely what, for his purposes, is meant by a realist. However, on p. 14 he informs us that

> "Realism is, of course, the belief in the existence of reality."

Reality – or "the world" – however

> *"...becomes that which exists independently of its being experienced, conceived etc..."*

The anti-realist cannot possibly wish to deny the first would-be realist tenet. However, he might say that the second does not, from any definition of 'reality' to which he might adhere, capture what he is at. Between them, the statements imply, to the anti-realist, that nothing (relevant) is real. Klausen's successive refinements of his definition 'realism' do not significantly alter the picture. He has defined the anti-realist in such a way that the latter must evaporate into the mists of vanishing ghosts. Despite his protestations to the contrary, Klausen does not seem to be too fond of his adversary. The anti-realist does not wish to maintain that there are no real things, or whatever. He expands on what 'reality' might mean.

Let me register a point of agreement with the author. Mark Johnston, Crispin Wright [Wright 1992], and others have revived Plato's old Euthyphro problem as an aspect of current debates over realism versus anti-realism in terms of so-called 'basic equations' of the following sort:

> (BE) a has F, if and only if a appears to be F to the standard observer in favourable circumstances.

It has been supposed that the realist with respect to properties like F ought to reject (BE); whereas the anti-realist, taking F to be response-dependent, emphatically embraces such equations. Indeed, perhaps anti-realism simply consists in this tender embrace. Typically, 'F' might be a colour predicate ('red') or the appellation of some morally relevant feature ('brave'). Klausen is absolutely right that equations like (BE) have no bearing on the realism/anti-realism issue, unless 'if and only if' is construed in some fashion other than that of the material biconditional. On the latter reading, any reasonable instance of (BE) will be acceptable to realist and anti-realist alike. Furthermore, it does not matter if we either complicate the conditional (much in the way Carnap attempted long ago with reduction sentences for sentences expressive of dispositional properties [Carnap 1936/37]) or insist that (BE) instances be a priori. It seems, though, that the latter point must be accommodated, if we are to articulate the Euthyphro contrast.

However, Klausen appears to leave the matter at the point of having deemed the equations irrelevant to the realism/anti-realism issue. This is a mistake. There is a clear-cut issue of direction of dependence involved. The anti-realist wishes to express that a is, say, red, because competent observers in favourable observers would agree that it is. This translates into a pair of counterfactuals (assumed to behave like Lewis-Stalnaker-Thomason conditionals, which do not admit of contraposition [Stalnaker 1968; Stalnaker & Thomason 1970; Lewis 1973a]):

(a) If favourably placed standard observers were to have looked at a and judged that a was red, then a would have been red.
(b) If favouably placed standard observers, on looking, would not have agreed that a was red, then a would not have been red.

In short, the property red tracks informed judgement. The realist in respect of colours wishes the tracking to go in the opposite direction. He therefore adheres to:

(c) If a had been red, then favourably placed standard observers would have agreed, on looking, that a was red.
(d) If a had not been red, then favourably placed standard observers would have agreed, when looking, that a was not red.

These pairs of counterfactuals aim to capture asymmetrical relations of dependence, on the pattern of David Lewis's analysis of counterfactual dependence [Lewis 1973b], which is also the model for Nozick's notion of tracking conditions. There is however in the present case no hint that the dependence in question is (qausi-)causal. After all, no anti-realist could possibly wish to maintain that surfaces turn red as a causal result of our looking at them. Such cases do occur: a virgin may blush under the sustained stare of an attractive male, and the change in colouring consequent to the cheeks of the virgin might well be captured by a suitable pair of Lewis conditionals. The kind of change of complexion involved in such cases is however 'real' in a manner such that the realist and the anti-realist will agree over its occurrence. Incidentally, this raises the time-honoured question concerning how to capture exactly causal dependence in terms of counterfactuals [Kim 1973]. The other side of the coin is how to capture different kinds of dependence by similar means. Refinements are called for.

For our purposes the beauty of invoking counterfactuals is that these, unlike material and strict conditionals, do not admit of contraposition. If they did, the pair (a) and (b) would be equivalent to the pair (c) and (d). In fact, either pair would be equivalent to

(e) a would have been red, if and only if favourably placed standards observers had agreed that it was.

The point of introducing counterfactuals is exactly to avoid this contrapositive collapse.

Counterfactuals hold a further attraction: they are not subject to Strenghtening of the Antecedent. So, I can assert

(f) If there had been snow, I would have gone skiing.

and yet not be committed to

(g) If there had been snow and an avalanche, I would have gone skiing.

Lewis-semantics for counterfactuals deal with such cases by showing how it may well be that I go skiing in all the nearest possible snowbound worlds, without it being the case that I go skiing in all the the nearest possible snowbound worlds with avalanches in them. So, counterfactual conditionality is non-monotonous. What is more, the work is done at the semantical level, as opposed to all attempts to capture the circumstances in which (f) is assertible by qualifying the antecedent or complicate syntactical matters in some other way. And this is why we do not have to negotiate the Carnapian way of dealing with basic equations to make them quite right.

Furthermore, the fact of 'red' being a vague predicate is disregarded in the above, as not being relevant to present concerns. The realist does not have to assent to (c) and (d). He probably will, on the strenght of taking these counterfactuals to derive from the meaning of (or even be part of the definition of) 'favourably placed standard observer'. The salient point is that the anti-realist is committed to (a) and (b) holding a priori, while the realist must reject this. According to the realist, (a) and (b) may well be true; but this would be by dint of epistemic luck. Hence, the Euthyphro contrast is genuine and does, *pace* Klausen, bear on the realism/anti-realism issue. The main interest of this is that the contrast concerns decidable sentences, hence sentences not in question within the Dummettian framework for staging the struggle between realism and anti-realism.

In the above, I have repeatedly complained that Klausen includes epistemological optimism in his definition of 'realism'. The provenance of this inclusiveness probably owes a great deal to recent, and not so recent, discussions of so-called 'scientific realism'. The latter denominates the doctrine that the physical world really is mind-independently more or less as current physics describes it; and this is clearly a dual doctrine about both ontology and epistemology. Quine thought this kind of realism to be tenable for quantum reality. Klausen goes along with this. But he wishes the doctrine to paradigmatically cover ordinary, middle-sized, dry goods as well. As pointed out in the above, now well-rehearsed troubles arise over how to reconcile common sense and physics. Even at a fairly elementary level it is far from clear how my desk can both be a swarm of atoms in what is mostly a vacuum, yet purport to be a solid particular requiring two well-grown men to shift it from one place to another. We seem to be facing a dilemma: Either the desk is really there, and the empty space with its atoms are theoretical constructs. Or the latter are there. But now the desk seems to be a construct. It is not that the problem is insoluble. However, Klausen does not solve it. He suffers from a surplus of ontological generosity which will allow him to admit the mind-independent existence of just about anything, however well it might, or might not, fit in with the furniture already in place. On the face of things, it seems that if reductionism is banned the choice must be between some version of emergentisk realism or, if I may so venture, anti-realism with respect to the physical world either at the microlevel or at the more pedestrian level of the bigger chunks of matter about our own size.

Klausen serves up a good deal of phenomenological analysis of the deliverances of perception and even the result of empirically investigating whether it is not the case that realism in respect of ordinary middle-sized, dry goods forms part of common sense. Concerning the latter: of course it does. But questionnaires might not be the way to go about it. As Klausen is well aware (345 pp.), this is reminiscent of the methodology of Arne Næss's empirical enquiry into whether or not the man in the street endorses the correspondence theory of truth [Naess 1949]. I should not be surprised if one could possible locate a nation of people who would rather die than admit that their spirits do not transmute into eagles on death. In fact, I can think of one. Furthermore, common folk cannot be expected to understand such questions out of context. If anybody does understand, the answer is no good: she has probably already been ruined by having acquired at least a BA in philosophy.

Phenomenology, thought of as the philosopher's reflective exercise, is however not to be dismissed lightly. But it has to be taken with a grain of salt. For instance, there is no doubt that my current perception of my desk presents the desk as completely independent of me. Or in phenomenologese: the desk presents itself as independent of me. It also presents itself as shaped, sized, structured, coulored, placed durably in surroundings (space and time), capable of sustaining the weight of my PC (causally efficient), fairly impenetrable (thing-like), etc. But it also presents itself as a well-known, pleasant object. I can hardly look at the desk without coming to think of my maternal grandfather, who personally manufactured it. It may even occur to me that I could auction it away for a few bob. And if it went missing, I should surely feel the nothingness of the lost desk no less keenly than Sartre felt pangs on the occasion of the missing Pierre in the café. The point being that phenomenology is where philosophizing begins, not where it ends. The immediate *Lebenswelt* suffers from a glut of stuff which either is not really there, is there only because we are, or even because I am.

Finally, the above barely scratches the surface here and there of Klausen's comprehensive, learned, and thorough essay on many aspects of the realism/anti-realism controversy. The author's accomplishment not only merits our applause: we owe it to ourselves to study his book with some care[1].

Note

1. I hope to have benefited from having had the opportunity to discuss some of issues raised in the above with Søren Harnow Klausen on the occasion of his talk to the Society for Philosophy and Psychology at the University of Copenhagen, KUA, on October 7th, 2004. A previous version of the present paper was discussed at a NAMICONA workshop at Hotel Koldingfjord, Kolding, on December 4th, 2004. I am grateful to the participants for comments then offered.

Literature (Classics not included):

Armstrong, D.M. (1997) *A World of States of Affairs* (Cambridge, Cambridge University Press).
Carnap, R. (1936/37) Testability and Meaning, in H. Feigl & M. Brodbeck (eds.) (1953) *Readings in the Philosophy of Science* (New York, Appleton-Century-Croft), pp. 47-92.
Davidson, D. (1974) On the Very Idea of a Conceptual Scheme, in D. Davidson (1984) *Inquiries into Truth and Interpretation* (Oxford, Clarendon Press), pp. 183-198.
Devitt, M. (1984) *Realism and Truth* (Oxford, Blackwell).
Dummett, M.A.E. (1963) Realism, in M.A.E. Dummett (1978) *Truth and Other Enigmas* (London, Duckworth), pp. 145-16.
Dummett, M.A.E. (1973) The Philosophical Basis of Intuitionistic Logic, in M.A.E. Dummett (1978) *Truth and Other Enigmas* (London, Duckworth), pp. 215-247.
Kim, J. (1973) Causes and Counterfactuals, in E. Sosa (ed.) (1975) *Causation and Conditionals* (Oxford, Oxford University Press), pp. 192-194.
Lewis, D. (1973a) *Counterfactuals* (Oxford, Blackwell).
Lewis, D. (1973b) Causation, in D. Lewis (1986), *Philosophical Papers*, Vol. II (New York/Oxford, Oxford University Press), pp. 159-172.
Lowe, E.J. (2002) *A Survey of Metaphysics* (Oxford, Oxford University Press).

McDowell, J. (1994/1996) *Mind and World* Cambridge, Mass./London, Harvard University Press).
Naess, A. (1949) Toward a Theory of Interpretation and Preciseness, in L. Linsky (ed.) (1952/72) *Semantics and the Philosophy of Language* (Urbana/Chicago/London, University of Illinois Press), pp. 248-269.
Nozick, R. (1981) *Philosophical Explanations* (Oxford, Oxford University Press).
Rasmussen, S.A. & Ravnkilde, J. (1982) Realism and Logic, *Synthese* 52, pp. 379-437.
Rasmussen, S.A. (1990) Supervaluational Anti-Realism and Logic, *Synthese* 84, pp. 97-138.
Rasmussen, S.A. (2004) *Dummettianske temaer* (København, Museum Tusculanum Press).
Stalnaker, R. (1968) A Theory of Conditionals, in E. Sosa (ed.) (1975) *Causation and Conditionals* (Oxford, Oxford University Press), pp. 165-179.
Stalnaker, R. & Thomason, R. (1970) A Semantical Analysis of Conditional Logic, *Theoria* 36, pp. 23-42.
Strawson, P.F. (1966) *The Bounds of Sense* (London, Methuen).
Wright, C. (1992) *Truth and Objectivity* (Cambridge, Mass./London, Harvard University Press).